Developing
Ambient
Intelligence

Proceedings of the First International
Conference on Ambient
Intelligence Developments (AmID'06)

W0036720

Springer
Paris
Berlin
Heidelberg
New York
Hong Kong
Londres
Milan
Tokyo

Professor Antonio Maña
Universidad de Malaga
Campus de Teatinos Computer
Science
Department ETSI
29071 Malaga
Spain

Volkmar Lotz
SAP Labs France
Le Font de l'Orme
805, avenue Maurice Donat
06250 Mougins
France

ISBN-10 : 2-287-47469-2 Paris Berlin Heidelberg New York

ISBN-13 : 978-2-287-47469-9 Paris Berlin Heidelberg New York

© Springer-Verlag France, Paris 2006
Imprimé en France
Springer-Verlag France est membre du groupe Springer Science + Business Media

SPIN : 119 06124

Maquette de couverture : Jean-François MONTMARCHÉ

Antonio Maña
Volkmar Lotz

Developing Ambient Intelligence

Proceedings of the First International

Conference on Ambient

Intelligence Developments (AmID'06)

 Springer

Preface

This volume constitutes the proceedings of research track of the First International Conference on Ambient Intelligence Developments, held in Sophia-Antipolis, France, during September 20-22, 2006.

The road to real AmI systems is full of obstacles in the form of very heterogeneous research challenges, belonging to many disciplines, but yet strongly related. Given the importance and the impact that AmI can represent in the society, all challenges related to AmI are receiving an increasing interest from the research community. At the same time for AmI technologies to become a reality we need a strong industrial support. Industry has also shown an important interest in AmI. Finally, government agencies, standards bodies, and decision makers are also a key element in this road to the materialization of the AmI vision.

The AmI.d conference has been designed to bring together all these stakeholders and to promote and disseminate the advances in technologies related or supporting the AmI vision. The focus of this edition of AmI.d is on the enabling technologies for AmI. In particular, the development of new software engineering and security engineering practices especially adapted to the new challenges introduced by AmI ecosystems. However, AmI.d also addresses all other aspects and faces of AmI, as shown by its very interesting and wide-ranging program.

In order to suit the needs and interests of the different communities, AmI.d has been structured into two different tracks:

- On the one hand, the "scientific track" was devoted to both theoretical and applied research, covers the most leading-edge research and contains contributions that have been formally reviewed and selected by a selected International Program Committee.
- On the other hand an "open track" was devoted to cover the industrial aspects, along with other aspects (social, economic, standardization and regulation, etc.).

The AmI.d progam was complemented by interesting activities, such as the AmI Labs tour, live demos and information booths and featured top-level keynote speakers and an interesting panel debate.

Finally, we would like to conclude this preface by expressing our gratitude to all people that contributed in some way to the creation of this conference, and through it to the creation of AmI.

September 2006

Antonio Maña
Volkmar Lotz
Program Co-Chairs
AmI.d'06

Organization

AmId is an international conference organized and implemented by Strategies Telecoms & Multimedia.

Executive Committee

Conference Chair:	Javier López, University of Málaga, Spain
Organization Chair:	Richard Briçaire, STM, France
Program Co-Chairs:	Antonio Maña, University of Málaga, Spain
	Volkmar Lotz, SAP Research, France

Organization Committee

Laurence Gissinger	STM, France
Lenick Perron	STM, France
Daniel Serrano	University of Málaga, Spain
Isaac Agudo	University of Málaga, Spain

Program Committee

Emile Aarts	Eindhoven Univ. of Technology, Netherlands
Julio Abascal	Universidad del Pas Vasco, Spain
Stefano Campadello	Nokia, Finland
Imrich Chlamtac	Create-Net, Italy
Jorge Cuellar	Siemens, Germany
Sabine Delaitre	JRC Seville, European Commission, Spain
Bertrand du Castel	Axalto, USA
Claudia Eckert	Darmstadt Univ. of Technology, Germany
Eduardo B. Fernandez	Florida Atlantic University
Paolo Giorgini	University of Trento, Italy
Christian Goire	Java Card Forum, INT
Sigrid Guergens	Fraunhofer SIT, Germany
Jordi Herrera-Joancomarti	Univ. Oberta de Catalunya, Spain
Martin Illsey	Accenture, France
Valerie Issarny	INRIA, France
Jan Juerjens	University of Bremen, Germany
Spyros Kokolakis	University of the Aegean, Greece
Brigitte Lonc	Renault, France
Jose-Manuel López-Cobo	ATOS Origin, Spain
Jianhua Ma	Hosei University, Japan
Andres Marín	University Carlos III of Madrid, Spain
Fabio Martinelli	CNR, Italy
Fabio Massacci	University of Trento, Italy
Gisela Meister	Giesecke and Devrient, Germany
Matteo Melideo	Engineering Ingegneria Informatica, Italy
Haris Mouratidis	University of East London, UK
David Naccache	Univ. La Sorbonne, France
Pierre Paradinas	CNAM, France
Pierre Plaza	Telefonica I+D, Spain
Joachim Posegga	University of Hamburg, Germany
Domenico Presenza	Engineering Ingegneria Informatica, Italy
Gilles Privat	France Telecom R&D, France
Carsten Rudolph	Fraunhofer SIT, Germany
Francisco Sánchez-Cid	City University London, UK
Ted Selker	MIT Media lab, USA
George Spanoudakis	City University London, UK
Kurt Stirewalt	Michigan State University, USA
Willy Susilo	University of Wollongong, Australia
Jean-Paul Thomasson	Eurosmart, France
Laurence T. Yang	St Francis Xavier University, Canada
Mohhamad Zulkernine	Queen's University, Ontario, Canada

VIII

Sponsoring Institutions

The present book could not have been published without the support of its exclusive sponsor : Philips Research

Table of Contents

X

Seamless Home Services*

Sebastian Feuerstack, Marco Blumendorf, Grzegorz Lehmann, and Sahin
Albayrak

DAI-Labor, Technische Universität Berlin
Secretariat GOR 1-1, Franklinstrasse 28/29, D-10587 Berlin, Germany
{Sebastian.Feuerstack, Marco.Blumendorf,
Grzegorz.Lehmann, Sahin.Albayrak}@DAI-Labor.de

Abstract. The growing number of smart devices providing services in
peoples' homes and the increasing number of services available via the
Internet creates two separate worlds that have not been successfully integrated yet. To bridge these two worlds, we propose a Home Service
Platform supporting the seamless integration of home-based and net-
centric services in a smart home environment. A common Service Engine supporting inter-service communication and aggregation provides
human accessible user interfaces via a Service Portal and allows representing devices through a Home Device Controller. The integration of
the two worlds allows us to create a new type of service: Seamless Home
Services.

1 Introduction

Peoples' homes are currently flooded with a growing number of intelligent devices providing more and more "useful" features. New smart home devices are
introduced as well as additional house control and telecommunication systems,
each loaded with numerous complex functions making the handling increasingly
difficult for end-users and developers. At the same time the number of available
net-centric services grows continuously, providing personalized and ubiquitous
access to information. These two environments are yet still separated, but there
is an increasing need for a new generation of services aggregating functionality
and integrating home-based and net-centric services. We call this new class of
services enabling access, configuration and usage in an intuitive way "Seamless
Home Services".

Seamless Home Services provide the end user with simple to use functionality
instead of hard to use device controls by concealing complex functionality in
adaptive user interfaces and automating repeating processes.

In this paper we present our solution for the easy provisioning of seamless
services in form of an integrated runtime environment, facilitating the work of
service engineers by bringing services and devices together in a straightforward
manner.

---

* The Seamless Home Services project is sponsored by the Deutsche Telekom AG.

The next chapter gives a summary of the related work in this area, followed by chapter 3 where we identify the challenges motivating the development of Seamless Home Services. Afterwards we describe our approach to face those challenges, the *Home Service Platform*, followed by chapter 5, introducing our home infrastructure and the services we implemented to test our approach. Finally chapter 6 summarizes our work and gives an outlook to future research work.

2   Related Work

The increasing number of home devices and home networks leads to heterogeneous home environments, consisting of different types of networks and incompatible devices. In the home automation area multiple vendor specific proprietary protocols compete with proposals for standardization like e.g. EIB, X10, OneWire and I2C or ZigBee and various standards like e.g. UPnP, DLNA, SLP, Jini and Havi have been proposed to enable interoperability between devices of different vendors. In addition, smart services for the home environment have been proposed on basis of OSGi [4] and several research efforts like UIUCs Gaia [14], Stanford's iROS [9] or MIT's Metaglue [5] aim for the development of platforms allowing service interactions based on software agents within intelligent environments. Several of the existing standards also try to address specific use cases for appliance aggregation [3] or service aggregation [15].

McGrath et al. describe a concept [11] to use semantic queries that refer to ontologies for a semantic service. The iCrafter service framework [13] focuses on an approach for automated service aggregation on the user interface level.

Different to these approaches, focusing on device control and device interoperability, we concentrate on the connection between home-based and net-centric services. We thus take the aggregation of services one step further and unite home-based device specific services and net-centric services considering three aspects: abstraction from device specifics, user interface integration and service interoperability.

3   Challenges

We identified three challenging objectives that our approach has to meet to unite the home environment with the services offered by the internet for the creation of Seamless Home Services:

Interconnecting devices

The first challenge to face is the integration of various devices from different vendors as our anticipated home environment has to be able to interact with the devices and services available in the home. This requires an open system allowing the integration of devices from different manufacturers, supporting different standards and communication protocols.

Merging home-based and net-centric services

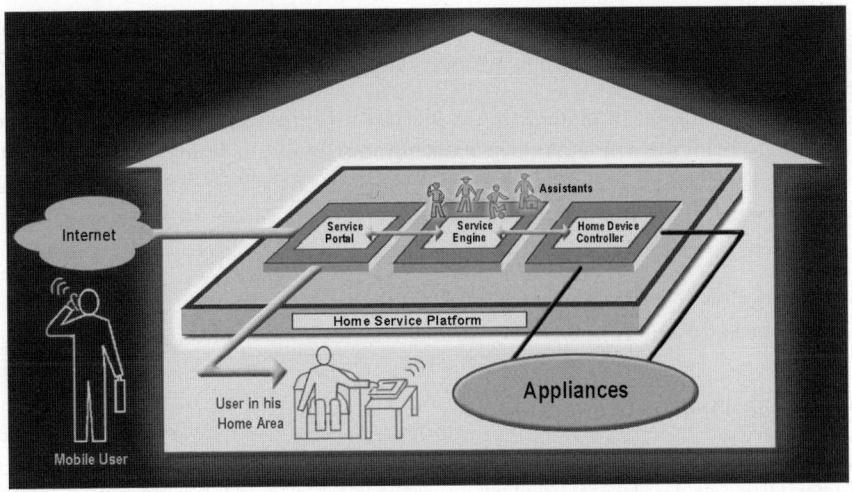

Fig. 1. Home Service Platform (HSP)

Once devices in the home are connected, the provided home-based services have to be merged with net-centric services to allow the provisioning of new and innovative services based on the available home infrastructure. This requires a home infrastructure mediating between home-based and net-centric services enabling both to expose their capabilities to each other.

Accessing services

Mediating between different services is one aspect of the anticipated architecture, mediating between the services and the user is another one. All provided services and devices have to provide a consistent user interface that can be personalized and integrated in the home environment, providing easy access to the various services.

Derived from these identified challenges, it appears that an integrated architecture uniting services, device controls and user interfaces is needed to benefit from the increasing range of functions and the convergence of modern devices and service providers. In the following we propose a solution for an architecture, targeting the identified objectives.

4   The Home Service Platform

We propose a common Home Service Platform (HSP) acting as a bridge between users and devices, providing the main service infrastructure in the home environment. This HSP aggregates the available services, supports developers with a common infrastructure for the integration of services and provides a common and consistent user interface to the end user. In our approach, the proposed Home Service Platform (3) consists of three building blocks, representing an architecture similar to a classic three-tier-architecture:

- A *Home Device Controller,* handling the discovery and control of devices and sensors at home and abstracting from the device specific protocols and networks.
- A *Service Engine*, implementing a virtual machine as service runtime environment bridging the currently existing gap between home-based and net-centric services.
- A *Service Portal*, providing unified and seamless access to services and devices.

In the following sections we give a more detailed description of the three building blocks of our Home Service Platform implementation.

4.1 Home Device Controller

The Home Device Controller (HDC) is the back-end of our architecture, responsible for discovering devices and the provided services and exposing these to the Home Service Platform. To provide a homogenous access to different home devices, we created an ontology, containing multiple categories representing devices with specific functionalities like sensors or power switches for example. These categories describe the functionalities of the devices and may be seen as device profiles creating an abstract layer encapsulating heterogeneous devices. This information is then used in various services to control the behavior of the home environment. To access devices the HDC encapsulates each connected device by a controller, responsible for the communication with the device via device specific mechanisms (i.e. UPnP, Jini, or plain HTTP).

The controller exposes the device capabilities via the device ontology which allows other services to access the devices in a generic manner. Changes of the device status are propagated via an eventing mechanism broadcasting status updates.

One of the main goals of our development was to ensure easy extensibility of the *HDC* architecture, to be able to easily integrate new device standards. We have provided means for integration of new controllers and device discovery architectures. On this basis, we have implemented support for numerous device types, based-on UPnP device profiles. Although the architecture is designed to integrate device specific services into the HSP, it is not limited to these. Any service can be encapsulated by a controller and presented to the system as a device which is directly accessible from the Service Engine to allow the easy integration of device functionalities into complex home services.

4.2 Service Engine

The Service Engine is our basic runtime environment uniting the Service Portal and the Home Device Controller to bridge the gap between home-based and net-centric services. It thus executes and manages the Seamless Home Services and offers a component-based approach to bundle services and enable remote administration and management. As we experimented with OSGi and Jini, we noticed that service interoperability becomes complex as soon as an unknown configuration of services at the target environment is considered. Thus, looking at scalability requirements, the loose coupling of components, and an elegant way for automatic services composition, we decided to implement a Service Engine that is driven by an agent environment [16].

Our Service Engine is based on the Java-based Intelligent Agent Component-ware (JIAC) [7] [16] [17], which is compliant to the FIPA agent management specification [6], defining an infrastructure consisting of an agent communication channel (ACC) (for inter-service communication), an agent management system (AMS) (allowing to address services and to control their lifecycles) and a directory service (DF) storing descriptions of available services. We refer to ontologies [8] in order to describe service functionalities such as their specific conditions, as well as their supposed effects. These descriptions are the basis for a partial-order planning algorithm [12] enabling the installed services to make use of new, yet unknown services. Currently we are using our Service Engine as a runtime environment for both, net-centric and home-based services, bridging the gap between home-based and net-centric services by allowing service concatenation and inter-service communication.

4.3   Service Portal

Access for human users to the services provided by the service engine is realized via a web-based Service Portal. The portal offers service access by aggregating service user interfaces into one consistent and unified home portal. Each service user interface is realized as a portlet based on a JSR-168 [10] standard provided via the Multi-Access Service Platform (MASP) [1] [2], which mediates between the services and the user interface representation. The MASP renders multimodal user interfaces for HTML, WML and VoiceXML-based browsers by processing an abstract XML-based interaction description. This abstraction layer allows delivering our user interfaces to a wide range of devices supporting voice and visual interaction. The portal-based approach allows the aggregation of service user interfaces making service and device control much easier for users. The device independence of the MASP approach ensures ubiquitously available services that adapt to specific situations of the user by allowing seamless switching between voice-based and graphic-based interaction depending on the users' specific situation.

In combination with the intelligent home environment and ambient utilities like localization services, device discovery and automated device selection, the described features provided by the Home Service Platform allow to increase the usability and automation of the home environment.

5   Seamless Home Services

To validate our approach, we set up a testbed that reflects a typical home infrastructure and allows merging home-based and net-centric services. We deployed

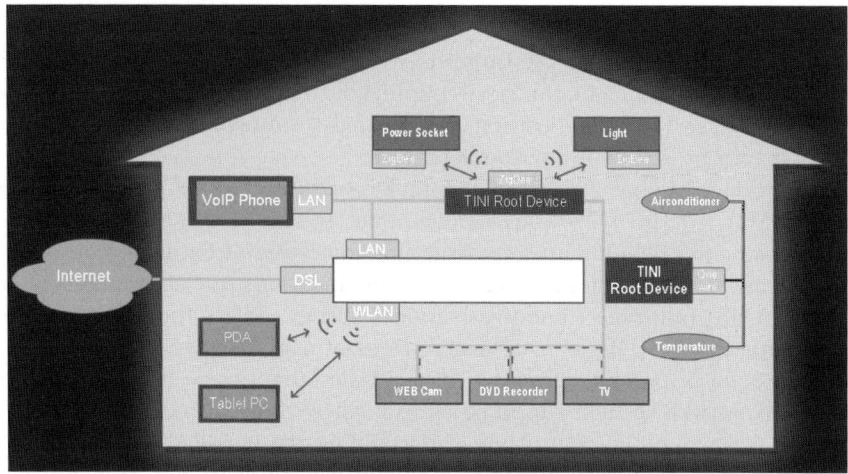

Fig. 2. Home infrastructure

the Home Service Platform presented in the previous section and implemented a set of services that seamlessly integrate into the home environment.

5.1   Home Infrastructure

Our home infrastructure testbed (5) consists of a central home server merging different types of networks, devices and services. It connects to the Internet on one side and to the home IP network on the other side. The home IP network transfers content and IP based communication (i.e. UPnP messages) and provides access to other home automation networks like OneWire and I2C bus systems. Proprietary networks like ZigBee, X10, EIB or OneWire are mapped to IP by using root devices as mediators. We implemented two reference root devices by using a TINI board that can be programmed using Java to map a proprietary protocol to our IP infrastructure. To create a realistic home environment we then connected different devices to our network including DVD recorders, TVs, cameras, computers (storing media files, etc.), handcrafted ZigBee-based controllable power sockets with devices, sensors and various terminal devices.

Based on this infrastructure we developed several Home Services, presented in the following section to test our implementation and to provide a controllable home environment as basis for further research activities in this area.

5.2   Implemented Services

To test our approach, we identified four service categories that we consider important for the residents of a home and implemented each service category by means of a software agent that can act on behalf of the user, as it knows about the user's preferences and is able to sense and control the user's environment.

All developed services have been aggregated in a home portal providing a central point and a consistent interface to unify the access to all home services (6).

A *Home Control Assistant* offers an integrated view of all appliances and sensors embedded in the home environment by using the Home Device Controller. All connected appliances can be controlled through the home portal via different connected devices, such as a PDA, a web browser running on a (tablet) PC or a voice based interface. The Home Control Assistant can be easily extended to integrate new standards for home automation which we tested by integrating various sensors, UPnP and ZigBee devices and some legacy systems for home automation.

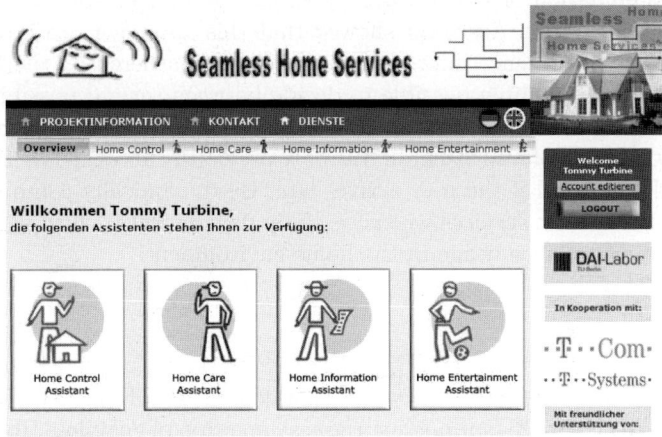

Fig. 3. Home portal

A *Home Care Assistant* is able to automate tasks on behalf of the user by allowing the definition of rules to control devices and services in the intelligent home. Rules basically describe actions to trigger if specific events take place. A scenario could turn on the TV and dim the light if it is after 8 o'clock, the user is in the living room and the news are on TV.

A *Home Entertainment Assistant* realizes a media control module, allowing the creation of media connections for A/V playback as well as a Personal Video Recorder (PVR) that can record movies on behalf of the user.

Finally, a *Home Information Assistant* implements a personalized news service for the home environment which continuously gathers information from the web on behalf of the user. Different from the other assistants, the Home Information Assistant is realized as a set of net-centric services, since it is a multi-user system that requires a high-bandwidth connection to continuously retrieve information and a lot of CPU power for its filtering algorithms.

Each assistant provides a value for the user on its own, but the power of our approach lies in the possibility to combine the services provided by the assistants. As all assistants are implemented on basis of our service engine, the Home Service Platform can now make the assistants aware of each other. Thus the Home Entertainment Assistant and the Home Information Assistant can be connected to learn from each other about the user's interests. In our prototype the Home Information Assistant is able to communicate with the Home Entertainment Assistant to program the users' personal video recorder to record films based on what the user likes to read about. The other way around, the Home Entertainment Assistant can give the Home Information Assistant feedback if and how long the user watched the recorded film, which is used to optimize user profiles for the personalized newspaper service. Further experimentation with the combination of Home Care Assistant, Home Entertainment Assistant and Home Information Assistant showed that this approach can be further extended. Based on presence information of the user, gathered by the Home Care Assistant it is for example possible to decide between several possibilities if the users favorite show is on TV. The show could be recorded if the user is absent, if could be directly played back on TV or a previously recorded or time shifted show could be played if the user arrives late. By dynamically combining home-based and net-centric services we successfully demonstrated, how we can gain a more convenient service usage in the home environment.

6   Conclusion

We realized a Home Service Framework that consists of a Home Service Platform and several basic services supporting the easy creation of Seamless Home Services and their integration into the home environment. Our approach combines three components, we identified as suitable to realize a comprehensive environment to support the creation of these services:

1. a Home Device Controller, allowing the integration of various home devices,
2. a Service Engine, uniting home-based and net-centric services,
3. a Service Portal, supporting multimodal access for users.

To test the feasibility of this approach we developed several services supporting the user in his daily life and successfully combined home-based and net-centric services. Our approach enables end-users to integrate net-centric services in their home environment allowing them to communicate with home appliances. This allows the development of Seamless Home Services that integrate well in the users' homes.

The connection between the services can further be used to enhance services with home-based information like the users position, information about the environment and the context of the service usage. We already started experimenting with localization infrastructure based on current state-of-the-art RFID and face detection technology to further enhance our demonstration environment, which works with simulated location information at the moment. The connection of this data to additional information about the home environment will allow us to better utilize available devices in the current direct neighborhood of the user.

During the work with the Home Service Platform in the home environment we also recognized the manifold possibilities that such a system provides for enhanced user interactions. In our future work we thus want to focus on the delivery of home services to the user via seamless multimodal user interfaces that easily integrate in the user's environment and utilize various available devices and modalities for user interaction. We expect our approach of a common Home Service Platform to be generic and comprehensive enough to provide the basic infrastructure necessary to realize ubiquitous and seamless access to services, net-centric or home-based, via adaptive multimodal user interfaces.

References

1. Andreas Rieger, Richard Cissée, Sebastian Feuerstack, Jens Wohltorf, Sahin Albayrak
"An Agent-Based Architecture for Ubiquitous Multimodal User Interfaces". *International Conference on Active Media Technology*, Takamatsu, Kagawa, Japan, 2005
2. Böse, J.-H. and Feuerstack, S., "Adaptive User Interfaces for Ubiquitous Access To Agent-based Services", *Agentcities ID3, Workshop on Human Agent Interaction*, 2003
3. Butler, M. H.: Using Capability Profiles for Appliance Aggregation. *IEEE International Workshop on Networked Appliances*, Liverpool, UK, October 2002
4. Chemishikian, S., Building Smart Services for Smart Home, 2002. *In proceedings IEEE 4th International Workshop on Networked Appliances*, pp. 215-224.
5. Coen, M., Phillips, B., Warshawsky, N., Weisman, L., Peters, S., Finin, P.: Meeting the Computational Needs of Intelligent Environments: The Metaglue System. *In 1st International Workshop on Managing Interactions in Smart Environments (MANSE'99)*, pp.201–212. Dublin, Ireland, December 1999.
6. FIPA 2000 Specification, FIPA Agent Management Specification [Online] from: ww.fipa.org, 2000. [Accessed 07/03/06]
7. Fricke, S., Bsufka, K., Keiser, J., Schmidt, T., Sesseler, R., Albayrak, S.: Agent-based Telematic Services and Telecom Applications. *Communications of the ACM*, April 2001
8. Gruber, T. R.. Toward Principles for the Design of Ontologies Used for Knowledge Sharing. *Technical Report KSL 93-04*, Knowledge Systems Laboratory, Stanford University, 1993.
9. Johanson, B., Fox, A.,Winograd, T.: The InteractiveWorkspaces Project: Experiences with Ubiquitous Computing Rooms. In *IEEE Pervasive Computing Magazine 1(2)*, April-June 2002
10. JSR-000168 Portlet Specification v. 2.1, October 2003 [Online] from: http://jcp.org/aboutJava/communityprocess/final/jsr168/ [Accessed 02/21/06]
11. McGrath, R.E., Ranganathan, A., Campbell, R.H., Mickunas, M.D., Incorporating semantic discovery into ubiquitous computing infrastructure, System Support for Ubiquitous Computing *Workshop at the Fifth Annual Conference on Ubiquitous Computing* (Seattle, WA),2003.

12. Penberthy, J. S., and Weld, D. S. 1992. UCPOP: A Sound, Complete, Partial Order Planner for ADL. *In Proceedings of the Third International Conference on Principles of Knowledge Representation and Reasoning (KR'92)*, 102-114
13. Ponnekanti, S., Lee, B., Fox, A., Hanrahan, P., and Winograd, T., ICrafter: A service framework for ubiquitous computing environments, *Ubicomp*, 2001, pp. 56–75.
14. Romn, M., Hess, C.K., Cerqueira, R., Ranganathan, A., Campbell, R.H., Nahrstedt, K.: Gaia: A Middleware Infrastructure to Enable Active Spaces. *In IEEE Pervasive Computing*, pp. 74-83, Oct-Dec 2002.
15. Sanders, R. T., Bræk, R., von Bochmann, G., and Amyot, D.: Service Discovery and Component Reuse with Semantic Interfaces. Springer-Verlag, A. Prinz, R. Reed, and J. Reed (Eds.): SDL 2005, LNCS 3530, pp. 85–102, 2005.
16. Sesseler, R.,"Building Agents for Service Provisioning out of Components", AGENTS '01, *Proceedings of the Fifth International Conference on Autonomous Agents*, 2001.
17. Sesseler, R., Albayrak, S.: Service-ware Framework for Developing 3G Mobile Services. *The Sixteenth International Symposium on Computer and Information Sciences, ICSIS XVI*, 2001

An Accessible Control Application for Domotic Environments

Dario Bonino and Alessandro Garbo

Dipartimento di Automatica
ed Informatica
Politecnico di Torino
Torino, Italy
{dario.bonino, alessandro.garbo}@polito.it

Abstract. In a future of smart, intelligent houses where multiple heterogeneous devices will be interconnected to provide new functionalities, to enhance user productivity and to ease everyday tasks, several issues will challenge the research community, including interoperability, communication, security, hardware and interfaces. The biggest challenge will probably be maintaining the focus on the user as the ultimate target of this intense research effort. The work presented in this paper, although in a small scenario, tries to maintain the user centrality in ambient intelligence by assisting people affected by degenerative diseases such as the Motor Neuron Disease in their everyday life at home. In particular, the paper proposes an eye/head-driven application that allows to control a domotic home through an almost-standard, already existing, house gateway. The ability to follow the user through all the stages of the disease, the adoption of low cost cameras for the tracking and the ability to easily control heterogeneous devices with a single "high-level" access point are the main innovation points.

1 Introduction

In a future of smart, intelligent houses where multiple heterogeneous devices will be interconnected to provide new functionalities, to enhance user productivity and to ease everyday tasks, several issues will challenge the research community, including interoperability, communication, security, hardware and interfaces. In the required, intense, research effort for reaching this future there is a sensible risk to lose the focus on the main target of developed solutions: the User. Researchers, as well as Public Institutions are quite aware of this risk and are promoting several initiatives aimed at mitigating this issue. As an example the European Community has explicitly posed the accent on user centred approaches by promoting the 6th framework call on "ageing ambient living societies", whose goal is to provide support for those research projects aiming at supporting elderlies and disabled people in their in-home everyday activities, thus extending the time during which they can live independently in their own homes. This paper adheres to this user-centred approach trying to support a particular class of disabled people to autonomously accomplish their everyday tasks, taking advantage of already existing smart home solutions. A simple eye or head driven application for controlling a domotic house is presented, which allows people affected by severe degenerative diseases such as the Motor Neuron Disease [1] to control their houses, until the little-most eye motion can be detected. The innovation points are from one side the ability to support with a unique environment the entire evolution of the disease and on the other side the ability to interact with every device available in a house, provided that the device can be remotely controlled (either through wires or wirelessly).

The paper is organized as follows: section 2 describes relevant related works on eye/head tracking and domotic systems, with a particular focus on eye and head tracking systems used as interfaces to ambient intelligence. Section 3 describes the basic principles and the assumptions on which the work is built. Section 4 details the architecture of the proposed application identifying the involved subsystems and highlighting the role played by each of them, while Section 5, describes more precisely the adopted interaction paradigms and the proposed gaze-controlled application. Implementation and deployment of the system is described in section 6, while section 7 discusses the first experimental results and the involved issues. Eventually section 8 drives conclusions and proposes some future investigations.

2   Related Works

Traditionally eye and head tracking aids have been developed for enabling people to communicate, even when more traditional means as the voice or the ability to write texts are disrupted by diseases or disabilities. In these cases, every residual ability of the user has to be leveraged for enabling communication.

Movements must be translated into speech or written text for communicating with other people, so tracking technologies have historically been targeted and correlated with "typesetting" applications, were people can write texts by moving their eyes or head on a "visual keyboard". In this kind of applications the tracking accuracy constrain the communication throughput and is usually strongly related with the quality of devices used to capture and process the eye and/or head images. For the eye tracker systems a good accuracy usually leads to very expensive tools (around 10.000-30.000 Euro) while for head tracking valuable tools have undoubtedly more accessible prices: around 500-1500 Euro, obviously the more the devices are accurate, the more they will be expensive.

Eye tracking systems such as VisionKey, Eyegaze, MyTobii and ERICA [2], that work with expensive infra-red cameras or low-cost head tracking systems such as SmartNAV [3], TrackIR [4] and Tracker Pro [5], can, for example, show on the computer screen a complete visual keyboard nearly as simple to use as the standard ones, but, of course with a much slower typing throughput (as in iKey [6], ECKey [7] and The Grid [8]). These highly accurate systems can also be combined with alternative typing facilities such as Dasher [9], allowing a quite high writing throughput, sometimes very close to that of physical keyboards.

When eye tracking systems are less expensive due to the adoption of low-cost cameras as in GazeTalk [10][2], their accessibility is increased, because the financial effort required to use the technology is much lower than in the former scenario. However low cost is traded-off by a minor accuracy that does not permit interaction through a complete keyboard, thus alternative visual layouts have to be designed as done in Uko II [11] and Gazetalk [10][2].

Finally, current literature reports some tools using eye or head interaction in domotics and ambient intelligence (Eyepliance [12]). In this scenario, interfaces are more devoted to control the household environment than to communicate, and require the user to gaze at the device that he/she wants to command. Clearly the underlying philosophy is to spread control over the whole home environment instead of centralizing it.

3   Basic principles

One of the main aspects in the definition of the quality of life of a human being is autonomy. Autonomy can be defined, in simple terms, as a person's ability to make independent choices. This independence can be independence of thoughts, i.e., the capacity of a rational individual to make an informed, uncoerced decision, physical independence, i.e., the capacity of a person to accomplish physical tasks, movements for example, in a self-determined manner, or other types of independence. In this paper we consider autonomy as the ability to self-determine the actions and the interactions with home appliances or furniture and with other people living in a household environment. This is a rather restrictive, physic definition of autonomy, however it is quite useful when end-users belong to those population categories that can have difficulties in motion and in controlling physical objects such as elderlies and people affected by motion disabilities.

The start point of the proposed approach derives therefore from situations in which being autonomous means, as first, being able to control an home environment and being able to communicate with other people. Since the communication problem has already been widely addressed and cost-effective, efficient solutions exist, this paper is focused on the ability for people to control their own home in spite of diseases, disabilities or age.

The first assumption made while developing the work defines the usage scenario, i.e. the group of users to which the proposed system is devoted. Final users, in this scenario, are able to use nothing but the head or the eyes to control their home environment. This is not a particularly strict or unrealistic assumption, in fact users can be: disabled people (people affected by the Motor Neuron Disease for example), injured people, elderlies.

In order to completely control a domestic environment through gaze or through head movements some facilities are needed for transforming user glances into commands and for physically actuating such commands. Two main technological components are needed: a eye/head tracking system and a domotic house. The eye/head tracker follows the user movements and maps these movements on to proper actions, by means of a control application. The domotic house executes the actions, closing the forward link of the user-home interaction loop (Figure 1). In the opposite direction, the house senses the environment and communicates its state to the control application which manages such information, possibly warning the user and requiring actions when needed.

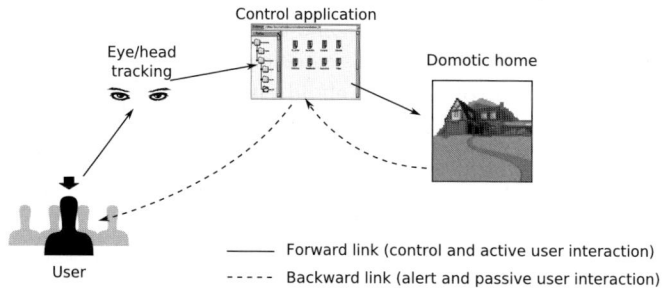

Fig. 1. The interaction loop between users and their homes.

Both technologies are not new in research so viable solutions can be identified quite easily and can be extended (when needed) for supporting all the required functions. Several trades-off can be taken, depending on the capabilities or features one may want to support. The main concern, in this work, is to define a usable and precise enough system while maintaining as low as possible the accessibility barriers of costs and integration capabilities. The design choices reflect this intention by selecting a head/eye tracker based on commercial, low cost web cams, and by adopting a house manager system able to interface different domotic networks such as the BTicino MyHome [6] or the EIB/KNX-based Siemens instabus [14]. In order to overcome the involved interoperability issues the house manager shall provide a common, high-level access to the devices connected to these networks.

The two systems are namely the Sandra eye and head tracker [15] and the house manager developed by the e-Lite research group of the Politecnico di Torino [7]. On top of them a control application has been developed from scratch, which implements several principles of usability and accessibility providing a suitable environment for issuing commands to a household environment and for checking the current state of the various devices available in the same environment. The high-level architecture of the resulting system is depicted in Figure 2.

4   System Architecture

Architecturally speaking, the proposed system is mainly composed of three elements, two of which already available, except for some improvements developed in the context of this work, and one entirely designed from scratch. They are

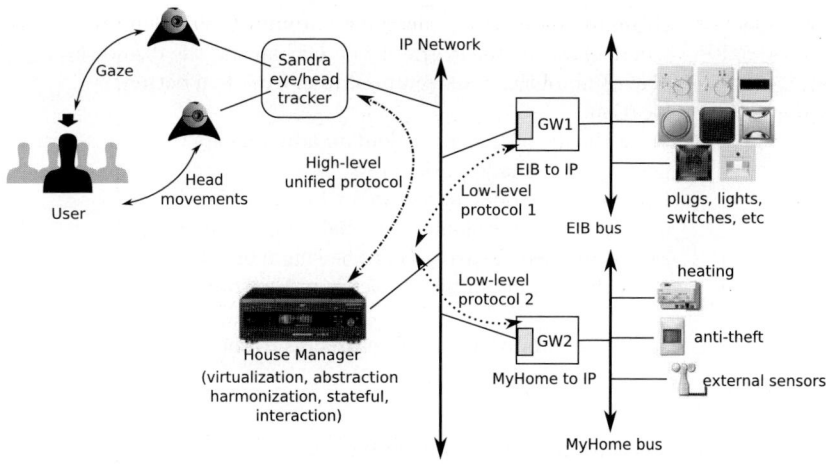

Fig. 2. The high-level architecture of the proposed system.

respectively the Sandra eye and head tracker, the house manager and the control application.

4.1 Sandra

Sandra is an eye/head tracking system developed by some of the authors, which supports gaze controlled interaction with computer applications through the adoption of low cost web cams. It is designed to explicitly address the issues related to degenerative diseases, in a effort to provide a single aid able to follow people affected by Motor Neuron Diseases in every stage of their impairment. So, in the first stages of the disease, where the users can still consistently move the neck muscles, the system is able to work as a quite accurate head tracker. Instead, when the disease gains ground and the user can only use the eyes, the system becomes an accurate enough, non-infra-red, eye tracker.

Sandra is based on a recognition algorithm for detecting head and eyes movements that directly stems from the Active Shape Model (ASM) algorithm [17]. The ASM is basically a contour detector, which allows to recognize shapes by identifying their boundaries, the eye for eye-tracking, or the intersection between the eye-brows and the nose for head-tracking.

The pure ASM, originally developed by Cootes (pseudo-code in Figure 3), is affected by some shortcomings in real time tracking applications, especially if images come from low-cost web cams. When the operating environment is noisy, in fact, web cams allow to capture only few accurate frames and, on these frames, the ASM encounters several difficulties since the features adopted for shape recognition (grey-levels) are affected by light conditions and other factors that likely change over the available images. The consequent variability in recognition accuracy is often too high for the tracking task, thus preventing the adoption of the pure ASM in home environments, which are noisy by nature.

> 1. Examine a region of the image around each point to calculate, with the gray-level mechanism, the displacement of the point required to move it to a better location.
> 2. From the displacements calculate adjustments to the position and shape parameters.
> 3. Update the model parameters: by enforcing limits on the shape parameters, global shape constraints can be applied ensuring that the shape of the model instance remains similar to those in the training set.

Fig. 3. The iterative run-time process of the ASM

In Sandra, these issues have been mitigated by slightly modifying the Cootes algorithm. Instead of grey-levels (which are strongly light-dependent), a new characteristic has been introduced called "colour-level" where the colour components (RGB) of pixels that are perpendicular to the object contour are recorded. The strip of pixels recorded for each shape landmark (the point on the shape contour used for training the recognition algorithm) is much wider than the one in the original ASM both in width and length. This makes the new algorithm more robust to light changes or channel saturations typical of images taken by low-cost cameras.

The prevision step of the ASM has also been modified in order to reduce the amount of iteration cycles required to find a given object. By using assembly instructions available for both Intel and AMD microprocessors (very fast execution) and by using a matrix representation of the image pixels, the required iteration steps have been reduced to 40-50 in comparison with the 100-120 of the original algorithm. This allows to more easily track the target object in every image captured by cameras. Improvements, unfortunately, do not come for free and while being more robust to light variations, the new algorithm is slightly more shape-dependent than the ASM. This, in the end, requires different calibration steps for the eye and the head tracker respectively.

In the eye tracking mode, eye shapes are captured as training images for the model and clustered into sets of similar images. Clusters are defined by the screen resolution of the system, fixed at 2 rows, each subdivided in 3 columns defining a total of 6 different clusters of colour-levels. The images are assigned to the clusters by requiring the user to fix at predefined points on the system screen and by capturing one or more snapshots of the user's eyes for each of these points. At runtime, when a new image is captured, the best matching cluster is identified by minimizing the distance measure between the colour-levels extracted from the captured image and the colour-levels that represent the centroid of each predefined cluster. One out of six clusters gets selected and drifts the next prevision step of the modified ASM towards the cluster centre.

In head tracking, instead, the shapes used as training set represent the several positions that the user's head can assume when he or she is gazing at the screen.

The user shall look to the outer edge of the system screen moving its head for calibrating the tracker. Captured head images are then elaborated to extract the domain of the head tracker, i.e. the head movements range that should be detected in the runtime tracking. All head positions falling outside the domain are interpreted as if the user is looking away from the screen. Due to the shape-dependency showed by the Sandra's modified ASM, accuracy of head tracking is much better than the accuracy of eye tracking. The shape recognized while tracking the head has in fact a central point, identified by the intersection of the eyebrows line with the nose line, which is quite easy to follow.

The Sandra architecture is completely modular allowing easy replacement or upgrade of the involved modules. Design has been strongly influenced by the two-folded nature of the system that acts both as an head and an eye tracker (Figure 4).

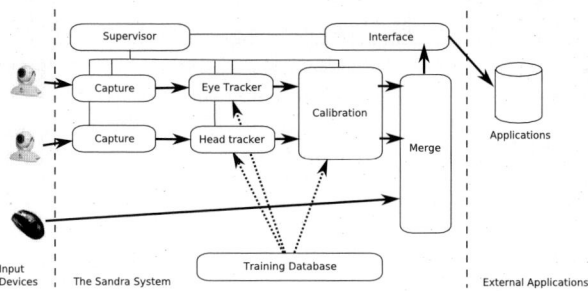

Fig. 4. The eye and head tracking system architecture.

Two main data streams are elaborated by the system: one for the algorithm in head tracking mode and the other for eye tracking. Eye, Head and Calibration modules make use of the Training Database module to store and retrieve the mathematical models and colour-levels they need for working. The Merge module uses the "gaze fixation" technique to select items and to interpret the pauses in the eye or head movements (dwell time) as the user's will to select what he/she is looking at. In addition, it collects relevant information from the system as the estimated accuracy, the user's gaze position and the detected selections and forwards them to the external applications by means of the Interface module.

Messages are designed to deliver information that could be relevant for the external applications business. Sandra can generate mouse and keyboard commands at the operating system level, as an example. Obviously these mouse messages will be more accurate in head tracking while in the eye tracking mode they can only target six areas on the screen. Planned improvements will combine the eye and head data stream in a unique data flow that will be elaborated at once using the head movements for compensating the offset of user's trembling or jerks, and exploiting all the user movements (head and eye) to make the framework more accurate.

4.2   The House Manager

In the proposed system the central point for interacting with the house environment is the House Manager. The House Manager is a concept developed by the e-Lite group of the Politecnico di Torino and presented at SAC 2006 [7]. Its structure (Figure 5) derives from standard house gateways being actively studied in the last years. The most interesting features, are the capability to "abstract" the home facilities using a high-level common language and the rule-based intelligence layer.

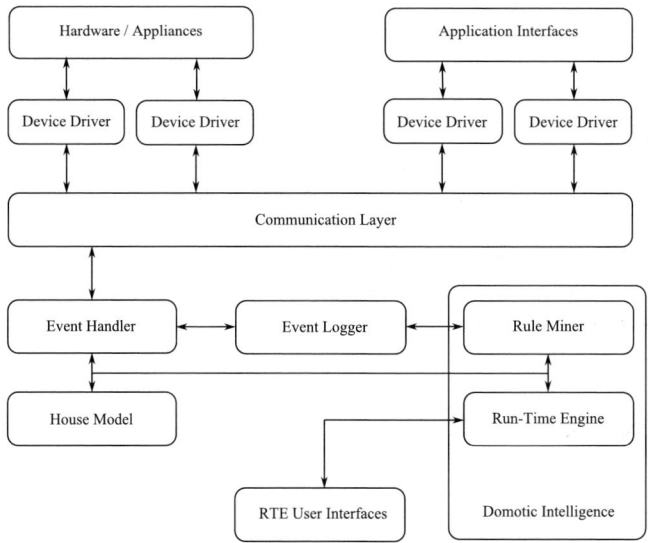

Fig. 5. The House Manager internal architecture.

The manager architecture, deployed as a standard OSGi framework, can be roughly subdivided in an abstraction layer and an intelligence layer. The abstraction layer, which includes the communication layer, the device drivers and the controlled devices/environments provides means for translating low level bus protocols into a common, high-level, human readable protocol that allows to uniformly access every domotic network and every home device, in a transparent manner. Such a protocol was originally developed from scratch, adopting a URI-like notation for devices and a predefined set of commands associated to each device type (see Figure 6 for some examples). This choice, while granting a uniform access to house components, independently from the available wired or wireless technologies, is however somewhat restricting, requiring manual configuration of the house setting for example, and adopting a too customized, possibly conflicting naming scheme. Therefore, while adopting the manager, the authors interacted with the manager design team (that works in the same lab) fostering the adoption of a more flexible protocol such as DomoML [18], including the semantic descriptions encoded by the DomoML-env and DomoML-func ontologies. This ensures, from one side the ability to virtually control all "electrically controllable" devices of a given household, and on the other side the ability to deploy the proposed system in different environments, with different settings, granting the desired accessibility level, at the hardware abstraction layer, at least.

The intelligence layer is composed by the modules that in Figure 5 lie below the communication layer. These modules allow to access domestic devices using an interaction model similar to that of human beings. The House Model for example, encapsulates the DomoML-env and DomoML-func ontologies and provides notions such as neighbourhood between controllable devices and furniture elements, abstraction of functional types of devices, etc. Using this model a user may issue a command like "shut down the light near the armchair in my bed room", or can issue a "light-up" command to a dimmer-driven light which usually has continue values of lighting that can range from 0 to 100%. The House Model is complemented by the Rule-Miner and the Rule-Engine that add some automated behavior to the Manager either by learning rules from the user behavior or by executing predefined rules. So, for example, one can set up a rule for blinking the light of the room in which he/she is located when the fridge gets switched off. In such a way he/she can avoid foods to deteriorate. In another case, the house may learn that the home temperature preferred by the house inhabitants is around 20 Celsius degrees and can automatically adjust the heating system to meet this preference.

$$kitchen.light.ON \tag{1}$$

$$lounge.CDPlayer.Play(track = 2) \tag{2}$$

Fig. 6. The URI-like high level communication protocol

5 The Control Application

The main focus of this paper is the control application that allows a user to fully interact with a domotic environment either through head movements or gaze. Target users are severely impaired people, in particular people affected by severe degenerative diseases like the MND that can evolve quite unpredictably both in time and in degree of impairment.

In order to follow the user through the entire course of his/her disease, the features of the Control Application shall respect some constraints. When the user has to adopt a different application layout due to the disease evolution, he/she shall not be compelled to learn a different way of interacting with the application. In other words, the way in which commands are issued shall persist even if the layout, the calibration phase or the tracking mode changes. To reach this goal the interaction pattern that drives the command composition has to be very natural and shall be aware of the context of the application deployment. For example, if a user wants to switch on the kitchen light, he/she goes in that room, then he/she searches the proper switch and finally confirms the desired change of the state actually switching on the light. This behaviour has to be preserved in the Control Application command composition and the three involved steps must remain unvaried even if the application layout changes according to the user condition.

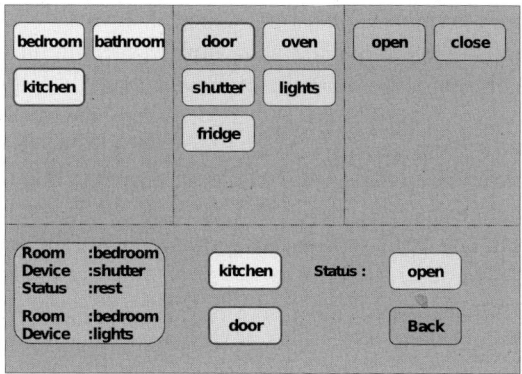

Fig. 7. The control application in the head tracking mode.

Two possible extremes define the adoption range of the Control Application: respectively, pure head tracking (maximum accuracy/resolution) and pure eye tracking (minimum accuracy/resolution). These two extremes evidently require different visual layouts, due to differences in tracking resolution and movement granularity. In the head tracking mode, Sandra is able to directly drive the computer mouse, thus allowing the user to select graphical elements as large as normal system icons (32x32 pixels wide). On the converse, in the eye tracking mode only 6 different screen areas can be selected (on a 1024x768 screen size this means that the selectable area is approximately 341x384 pixels). As a consequence, the visual layout cannot remain the same in the two modes, but the interaction pattern shall persist in order to avoid the user to re-learn the command composition process, which is usually annoying and reduces user satisfaction.

As can easily be noticed by looking at Figures 7 and 8 the two layouts are visually poor and use high contrast colours to ease the process of point selection. The main difference is the amount of interface elements displayed at time that results in a lower selection throughput for the eye-tracking layout.

The complete interaction pattern implemented by the Control Application can be subdivided in two main components referred to as active and passive

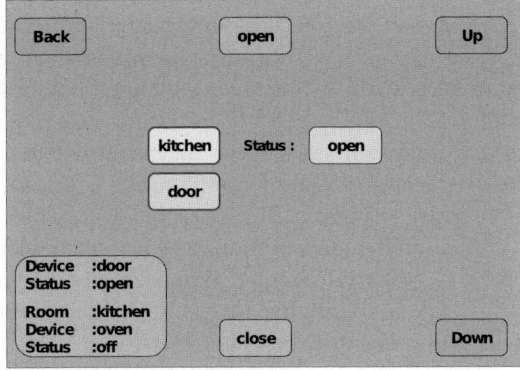

Fig. 8. The control application in the eye tracking mode

interaction. The former takes place when the user wants to explicitly issue a "command" to the house environment. Such a command can either be an actuation command (open the door, play the cd, etc.) or a query command (is the fridge on?,...). In both cases, "active" is referred to the explicitness of the user willing to which corresponds a measurable user action: eye or head motion.

The second part, instead is related to alert messages and to the general perception of the house status. Alerts must be managed in way that the user can timely notice what is happening and can timely offer the proper response. They are passive from the user point of view since the user is not required to actively perform a "check" operation, polling the house for possibly threatening situations. Instead, the system pro-activity takes care of them. House state perception, on the other hand, shall be passive as the user cannot query every installed device to monitor the current home status. As in the alert case, the Control Application shall provide a means for notifying the user about state changes in the domestic ambient, using a simple text banner, for example.

The following subsections better detail the problems involved in both the active and the passive parts of the interaction pattern as well as the solutions adopted in the presented work.

5.1   Active user-application interaction

According to the Fraser and Gutwin studies [19], the point and select interaction works through 3 different stages: cursor localization, cursor movement and selection. They shall be completely supported by the Control Application to make the interaction efficient, and satisfactory.

In the first stage the user looks at the screen to find the current cursor position. In eye-tracking, cursor localization is trivial since the cursor pointer follows the user gaze around the screen surface, being the selectable areas a priori defined and reduced in number. Instead with the head tracker, identifying the mouse position is a little more complicated.

In a normal mouse-based interaction, sometimes happens that the cursor arrow gets lost on the screen surface. A common interaction pattern for re-finding the cursor, adopted by almost all PC users, is to shake the mouse or to point the mouse to a known direction, the upper left corner for example. To support this step in head tracking the active-interface uses high-contrast colours that are able to naturally emphasize the cursor, thus simplifying the detection. However, when the cursor cannot be localized easily, a successful interaction pattern requires the system to promote a proper action that eases cursor detection. This action consists, in the Control Application, in requiring the user to fix the screen centre. In this condition, the system is able to sense the "cursor lost" situation and autonomously moves the cursor towards the screen centre for being located by the user.

Such a solution can sometimes appear al little bit redundant since, if head tracking works as eye tracking, the cursor shall follow the user's head movements. Unfortunately practical experiences showed that in head tracking cursor locking to head movements can easily be lost, due to latency in the elaboration of tracking data, and the most straightforward pattern for recovering this situation, is the one above described.

Once the user has located the cursor, the movement stage takes place and the cursor follows the head or the eye movement towards the target interface item. Since tracking is computationally intensive, this process can sometimes be slightly unresponsive. Therefore the user shall take confidence with the system for a while, before being able to quickly move the cursor across the screen. Experimental evidence shows that this skill can be acquired by almost all users in very few minutes.

The last stage is selection; this is a quite critical stage since the application is required to discriminate whether the user is fixing at a given visual element or is just looking around. In this case the best known solution in literature is to present some feedback to the user in order to warn him that a selection is being performed. Depending on the application, visual, auditory and tactile feedbacks can be used; in the proposed application, in particular, a progress bar is provided as the users are surely capable of receiving visual feedback.

Fig. 9. An example of selection visual feedback.

In all the three stages of the "point and select" process the user interface provided by the Control Application is grounded on a well known recall technique called Mental Map. This technique allows humans to record the location of items of interest in their field of sight [20]. It is a everyday evidence that almost all people after a brief exposition to a given image can easily remind the position, colours, and physical shapes of items occurring in the image. Image features that allow users to recognize a given object by gaze are called landmarks and are the basis of the Mental Map technique. If a user knows that a red button (the landmark is the red colour) lifts up the room shutters then he/she only have to spot the red zone on the screen to find out the shutter button.

Landmarks are adopted, in the Control Application, for easing navigation and selection of functionalities on the house interface, especially by defining a well established colour code that persists through all the application evolutions and adaptations. The user shall therefore memorize the corresponding Mental Map only at the beginning of the tool lifetime, which is designed to be as long as the user disease evolution.

Selection sequences are also used as landmarks, so, without regarding the system operating mode, if the kitchen is the first room in the house and the door is the first device in the kitchen this order is always preserved.

5.2   Passive user-application interaction

The underlying assumption of the head and eye tracking systems is that the user is not visually impaired, otherwise tracking the eyes would not be necessary. Therefore it is possible to exploit this user ability for showing information that can integrate and complete the tasks that the application allows to perform.

Especially in the eye tracking mode, where the selectable items are few, a great amount of screen space can be used for contextual information or for spot-like information about the environment, displaying the status of house devices for example. In such a way, the user awareness of the environment and of other people living in his/her home can be improved and threatening situations can be addressed. As an example, the presence of somebody knocking at the main entrance or an intrusion inside the house can be easily detected by an ambient intelligence system and can be reported by the Control Application as a visual alert, thus allowing the user to take the proper decisions: open the door or call the 911.

Status of house devices is also a suitable information to push to the user, so relieving him/her from the heavy burden of issuing a specific command whenever he wants to know if the fridge is on (as an example).

Care must be paid, however, when designing this kind of proactive visual interfaces. As the sight is already heavily loaded by the gaze tracking interaction, designers shall avoid to further overload this sense by continuously providing intrusive, annoying information. In order to avoid this shortcoming, the Control Application adopts a priority based alerting mechanism: in normal operating conditions, status information is displayed on a scrolling banner, similar to those of CNN TV-journals. The banner is carefully positioned on the periphery of the visual interface avoiding to capture user's attention too much and is kept out of the selectable area of the screen to avoid so-called "Midas Touch" problems [21] where every elements fixed by the user gets selected. In addition, the availability of a well known rest position for the eyes, to fix, is a tangible value added for the interface, which can therefore support user pauses, and, at the same time, maximize the provided ambient information. Every 20 seconds a complete check cycle warns the user about the status of all the home devices, in a low priority fashion.

Whenever a high priority information (alert) has to be conveyed to the user, the banner gets highlighted and the Control Application plays a well known alert sound that requires immediate user attention. In such a case, the tracking slowness can sometimes prevent the user to take the proper action in time. So, the banner has been designed to automatically enlarge its size on alerts, and to only provide two possible responses (yes or no) for critical actions. As only two areas must be discriminated, the selection speed is sensibly increased and, in almost all cases the user can respond timely to the evolving situation.

6   Implementation

The complete platform on which the Control Application has been deployed includes different modules, each deployed in a programming language that depends on the goal of the module itself. In particular the Sandra eye and Head tracker has been developed in the Windows environment using C++ and assembler for INTEL and AMD CPUs. This choice is related to the solution accessibility since a Windows based system that uses low-cost web cams is more accessible than a Linux/Unix based system, which usually lacks of correct drivers for such devices. This is especially true when considering the diffusion of the two operating systems in the market of low-skilled users.

The proposed Control Application is related with the Sandra system since they should interact to capture the user eye and head actions and to convert them into commands. Therefore also the control application has been developed in C++ in a Windows environment, however it can also be used by other available trackers. Conversely the House Manager, which was already available, and that shall be capable of communicating with different systems, each implemented in different technologies adopts a Java-based technology.

In the experimental setting the Control Application, and the Sandra tracker as well, have been deployed on a Windows based, i586 class PC equipped with 512 MByte of RAM. The House Manager, instead ran on a Linux-based, i586 class PC equipped with 1 GByte of RAM. Devices available for practical experimentation include a domotic system produced by BTicino (a leading Italian Industry for house electrical furnitures), an open source music server [22] and a hand-crafted led interface directly connected to the PC running the manager.

7   Experimental results

The active part of the AID control application uses a point and select approach that is quite similar to the ones adopted for standard users. However even the more intuitive pointing devices can show limitations and can generate problems if used by disabled people. Unfortunately, sometimes it is not possible to set up a benchmark that involves the final users, especially when the system under test is an active research work. In this case literature shows that it is possible to simulate the troubles that a disabled person can find in using the application by forcing the normal users to operate in stressful conditions.

This approach for example was adopted by Fraser and Gutwin [19] in their work where, to simulate a visually impaired person, a normal user was constrained to look at a screen from a very far point, thus inducing a situation actually near to the one of a low vision user.

According to this technique, the Control Application experimentation has been carried by non-impaired people (the authors and their colleagues in the e-Lite research Lab) forced to operate in conditions similar to those of target users. For example, in eye tracking trials, the authors used a semi-rigid cervical collar that limits the mobility of the neck, thus simulating a person that can only move the eyes. The same applies for head tracking, were the body movements were strictly controlled so as to simulate a person that can only move neck muscles. Of course results are not as valuable and convincing as if experimentation was carried by final users, however it must be noted that the application is still under refinement and the test-correction-test iteration time required by on the field experimentation, in this scenario, is too high. More extensive experimentation is already planned for the final development phase, possibly leading to a successful exploitation of the proposed system in the everyday life.

Experiments involved respectively the active and the passive user-application interaction provided by the Control Application.

In the first test a qualitative evaluation of the active interaction pattern has been performed. The evaluation has been based on the observation of the testers' behaviour while performing the experiments. User mumbling, gestures, etc. have been recorded as possible indicators of accessibility problems. Results show that the Control Application actually allows to manage the house devices through eye or head tracking. Accessibility assessment results have been satisfying for 7 out of 10 testers. The remaining 3 complained about the slowness of interaction in the eye tracking mode. However such complaints cannot be validated without test fields with impaired people, since testers were accustomed to the more efficient interfaces available to "normal users", so feeling the eye-based interaction slow.

The second test is as qualitative as the first, and aims at evaluating the effectiveness of the passive part of the Control Application. Both the house state perception and the alert management have been tested, using the ringing of the door bell as alert event. Testers have been required to timely respond to the alert, by opening the door.

As in the former test, the testers have been observed for detecting possible accessibility problems. In this case results have been nearly as good as for the direct interaction: 6 out of 10 testers have in fact been completely satisfied. The others, instead, newly complained about the slowness of the direct interaction required to open the door. On the validity of these last results can be provided the same comments provided in the former test, however the experiments showed that, by enlarging the banner text and by providing only a yes/no question to the user this problem can be addressed, obtaining as a result a positive judgement from all the involved people.

8   Conclusions

This paper presented a Control Application that uses eye and head tracking as a means for allowing not only communication but also interaction of severely impaired people with the environment that surrounds them. Results are still preliminary, however they provide some positive feedback on the feasibility of the approach and on the capability, of the application, to improve the nowadays interaction between disabled users and houses. Several issues need further improvements, as the presented work is still under development. Future works will improve the user-application interaction in terms of responsiveness, providing as result a platform ready to be tested by end users. To set-up this more extensive experimentation campaign the authors are already collaborating with care-givers institutes [23], in the context of the COGAIN European network of excellence [2].

9   Acnowledgements

This work has been partially funded by the European Commission under the EU IST 6th framework program, project 511598 "COGAIN: Communication by Gaze Interaction". The sole responsibility of this work lies with the authors and the Commission is not responsible for any use that may be made of the information contained therein.

References

1. MND association of victoria. http://www.mnd.asn.au/morefacts.html.
2. COGAIN: Communication by gaze interaction network. http://www.cogain.org/.
3. SmartNAV. http://www.zygo-usa.com/smartnav.htm.
4. TrackIR. http://www.naturalpoint.com/.
5. Tracker Pro. http://www.madentec.com/.
6. Raiha K.J. Majaranta P. Twenty years of eye typing: Systems and design issues. In *Proceedings of the ETRA 2002 symposium*, pages 15–22, New Orleans, Louisiana.
7. Instance H.O. Bates R. Zooming interfaces! enhancing the performance of eye controlled pointing devices. In *Proceedings of the ASSET 2002 conference, The Fifth ACM conference on Assistive Technologies*, Edimbourgh, Scotland, July 8-10 2002.
8. The grid. http://www.widgit.com/products/grid/index.htm.
9. The dasher project. http://www.inference.phy.cam.ac.uk/dasher/.
10. Johansen et Al. Language technology in a predictive, restricted on-screen keyboard with ambiguous layout for severely disabled people. In *Proceedings of the EACL 2003 workshop on Language Modelling for Text Entry Methods*, Budapest, Hungary, April 13 2003.
11. Garbe Jorn Kuhn Michael. Predictive and highly ambiguous typing for severely speech and motion impaired users. In *Proceedings of the UAHCI 2001 conference on Universal Access in Human Computer Interaction*, New Orleans, Louisiana, August 5-10 2001.

12. Roel Vertegaal et al. Media eyepliances: using eye tracking for remote control focus selection of appliances. In *CHI Extended Abstracts*, pages 1861–1864, 2005.
13. The BTicino MyHome system. http://www.myhome-bticino.it.
14. The konnex association. http://www.konnex-knx.com.
15. A. Garbo F. Corno. Multiple low-cost cameras for effective head and gaze tracking. In *Proceedings of 11th International Conference on Human-Computer Interaction*, Las Vegas, USA, July 2005.
16. F. Corno P. Pellegrino, D. Bonino. Domotic house gateway. In *Proceedings of SAC 2006, ACM Symposium on Applied Computing*, Dijon, France, April 23-27 2006.
17. T.F. Cootes et al. *Active Shape Models - their training and applications*, volume 61. 1995.
18. Francesco Furfari, Lorenzo Sommaruga, Claudia Soria, and Roberto Fresco. DomoML: the definition of a standard markup for interoperability of human home interactions. In *EUSAI '04: Proceedings of the 2nd European Union symposium on Ambient intelligence*, pages 41–44, New York, NY, USA, 2004. ACM Press.
19. Julie Fraser and Carl Gutwin. The effects of feedback on targeting performance in visually stressed conditions. http://www.graphicsinterface.org/proceedings/2000/, May 15-17 2000.
20. Amy Skopik Carl. Finding things in fisheyes: Memorability in distorted spaces. http://www.graphicsinterface.org/proceedings/2003/, June 11-13 2003.
21. Karn K.S. Jacob R.J.K. *Eye Tracking in human computer interaction and usability research: Ready to deliver the promises*, pages 573–605. 2003.
22. MServ a free, open source jukebox. http://www.mserv.org.
23. Molinette hospital. http://www.molinette.piemonte.it.

Learning and adaptive fuzzy control system for smart home

Vainio A.-M., Valtonen M., and Vanhala J.

Tampere University of Technology, Institute of Electronics
P.O. Box 692, 33101 Tampere, Finland
{antti-matti.vainio, miika.valtonen, jukka.vanhala}@tut.fi

Abstract. Automated smart homes have widely established their position as a research field during the last decade. More and more context sensitive concepts are being studied and at the same time proactivity has broken through in ambient intelligence research. Technology has advanced towards an adaptive and autonomous home, which can take care of the inhabitants' well-being in numerous ways.

We propose to use a context sensitive and proactive fuzzy control system for controlling the home environment. Since humans communicate using fuzzy variables, we see that applying context recognition to a fuzzy control system is straightforward. The designed control system is adaptive, and it can accommodate to changing conditions of inhabitants. Our system is designed to operate fully in the background and needs very little effort from its users. The system utilizes a principle of continuous learning so that it does not require any training prior to use.

This paper describes a lighting control system implemented using the fuzzy control system designed. We concentrate on the basic operation of such systems and present findings from the design process and initial tests.

1 Introduction

Imagine someone living in a smart home equipped with a context sensitive and adaptive control system. Most of the time the home is able to react correctly to the actions of the resident or take proper proactive actions, both based on a world model and measured variables. Inevitably at some stage the system makes an error and the resident has to take a corrective action. This enables the system to update its world model in order. Two research questions rise from this simple scenario: How to construct and update a world model? And how can the system differentiate between a corrective interaction and normal behavior of the resident. Our system answers these questions by utilizing context recognition and fuzzy control.

Context recognition is an effective method for providing application-specific information and enabling context triggered actions [1] [2]. It can be used for creating intelligent environments, and by utilizing machine learning algorithms with context recognition proactive systems can be established. [3] [4] Adaptive homes have been built by using context recognition [5] [2] and neural networks as a learning mechanism. A context-aware home can serve its inhabitants more flexibly and adaptively [4]. Context recognition deals with fuzzy quantities of environment, like warmth, brightness and humidity. Humans also perceive their environment with fuzzy variables [1]. Therefore, we see that a fuzzy control system would be suitable for controlling the home. Although the context-aware neural networks, which have already been utilized, can be converted to fuzzy systems, the implementation of a fuzzy system is much easier [6]. Moreover, by utilizing fuzzy systems for controlling the home and as a pre-processing and context learning mechanism, we believe that a more genuine and natural environment can be achieved.

We have developed a fuzzy control system that can learn its rule table without any predefined information and doesn't need any training prior to use. It can add and remove rules and modify existing ones based on learned information. With this versatile learning ability, we see that the control system can become unnoticeable after its initialization. Our implementation consists of a lighting control system that is implemented into a smart home.

1.1   Background

Smart environments have long been researched at the Institute of Electronics. Different technologies for smart spaces and their devices, networks, user interfaces and software solutions have been studied extensively in different projects. [7] The first smart space constructed was Living room, a former laboratory converted into a living room with small kitchen and a hall. The eHome-project took testing smart spaces to another level with ordinary people living in a smart apartment equipped with smart appliances and control for a long period of time. These studies highlighted the need for a control system that could learn from the behaviour of its users and use that information to adapt to people's needs without explicitly configuring the system. In other words, it would make the home actually feel smart.

In the study we focused on fuzzy systems, because they are well suited for dealing with imprecise quantities used by humans. Fuzzy systems are fairly easy to understand and construct, because they are based on natural language. The construction of the rule base in fuzzy systems is also quite easy to automate, because the method using natural language is simple to turn into a computer program. Control systems using fuzzy logic are generally fast, user friendly, cheap and they don't need much memory. [8]

We decided to use a lighting system as a prototype, because its operation could be easily observed visually and we had an existing infrastructure for such a system. The infrastructure allowed us to fully concentrate on developing the fuzzy control system instead of hardware components. The prototype was built to be an integral part of the smart home laboratory that is used as a testing space for new technologies.

1.2   Objectives

The starting point of the research was to study modelling of the dynamic behaviour of a home environment using fuzzy logic. A key element was to find algorithms to adapt the designed model to changing situations. After the design process we intended to create a control system for a smart home test environment. The study focuses greatly on context-based control and on learning process with fuzzy control.

The objective for this control system was to build a fuzzy architecture that would support learning from user actions and proactively anticipate users' needs based on the learned data. From the early stages of the control system design, one major target was to keep the system as unobtrusive to a home's inhabitants as possible. This of course determined that we would have to use user-friendly sensing methods and user interfaces. At the end of the study we aimed to validate the system with functional and user tests.

The study began from the premise that no predefined rule base, however intelligently and thoroughly devised, can possibly suit for everyone. Our habits and needs are just too different. Therefore the only one who can make a good rule base for a given user is that user himself. To accomplish this, inhabitants' actions would have to be monitored, and system would have to learn through these observations. The learning process would need to be continuous, because our habits and routines change over time.

Another objective for the system was that it would have to need minimum effort from the inhabitant. The less the inhabitant has to know about this system, the better. This objective benefits from systems continuous learning process, as it doesn't need a specific teaching mode or period. Also the system would have to need a minimum number of specific controls in addition to normal controls for lights and Venetian blinds. Small number of controls does not imply lack of control though. The inhabitant has to have the ultimate control over his home. Therefore the inhabitant has to have a chance to override all decisions that the fuzzy system makes.

The designed system should have two different control modes: autonomous control and event-based control. Autonomous control would have total control of the environment and it would anticipate users' needs based on the learned information. Event-based mode would react to inhabitant's overrides and enable system to trigger chains of controls based on immediate user actions. These two control modes would enable the system to flexibly adapt itself to the users' needs.

In addition the system was designed to be fairly easy to implement and existing infrastructure was to be used where applicable. In practise this meant that the system would be built on a software platform already in place in the smart home. It would also need to be easily modifiable to other areas than lighting. If a new system would be needed, it should be enough to define input and output devices with their membership functions.

2   Methods

2.1   Research facilities

The smart home laboratory was built during the eHome-project in 2002-2004, and it is located in the Institute of Electronics facilities. This smart home is a 60 m^2 apartment with some special modifications to help make technology invisible. It has removable floor and ceiling tiles, lots of space for equipment and customized electrics, which allow us to reconfigure lights, wall sockets and switches as needed. A picture of the smart home is shown in figure 1.

Fig. 1. The smart home

The smart home is equipped with various devices and technologies, including several wireless communications networks, host of sensors that monitor conditions of the apartment, motorised curtains and front door, fingerprint scanner, infrared tag ID and positioning system and a speech recognition system. All this is hidden from the user as well as possible, so that technology remains invisible until it is actually used. To make the apartment look and feel comfortable it is furnished just like a normal apartment. [9]

The user can control the smart home through various user interfaces (UI). There are many different kinds of user interfaces, as no interface is convenient in every situation. Provided control methods are a tablet PC, a mobile phone, TV and a speech recognition system. All interfaces connect to the home controller server that acts as a central gateway for the user interfaces and the devices. The server is connected to all devices of the apartment through different network technologies. Home controller offers a set of services to UIs, such as constant stream of up-to-date information of conditions in the home, grouping services for devices, timers and a logging service. Home controller is designed to work as a platform, on which intelligent services can be built by specializing certain classes. [10] The fuzzy system prototype was built this way. This way we were able to use the entire existing infrastructure in the smart home with minimum effort.

2.2   Simulations

Prior to implementation the fuzzy system was tested in a special simulator, which has a simple model of all of the system components. The simulator is a computer program with a user interface that enables us to monitor the system's operation at run time. This way we could first verify that the prototype was viable. The simulator was also very handy because it had a feature that allowed us to simulate passing of time with an accelerated rate. This saved much time in early stages of testing. The simulator is quite simple to configure for individual test arrangements and it could easily be used with other systems besides the lighting prototype.

2.3   Fuzzy systems

Since human speech and communication use fuzzy variables that have inexact bounds, fuzzy systems present an easy way to communicate between humans and computers. We propose that by using fuzzy systems a more natural and realistic environment can be established.

Fuzzy logic Fuzzy systems theory is based on uncertainty and on imprecision. Uncertainty is very natural to humans and people usually make decisions based on indiscrete observations. [8] A man can reason that he will not need an umbrella when going outdoors, if it does not rain much. Here the meaning of the fuzzy word 'much' is dependent on context and from the point of comparison.

The presentation of uncertainty is complicated to a computer using traditional methods. Among scientist uncertainty has been considered to be an inevitable part of speech and a precise expression has been an objective of research for a long period of time. [8] For example, for a computer it is very hard to understand what dark and bright means. Let us define a border between dark and bright to 100 luxes. If the sun shines outdoors, the illumination can be measured to be 50 000 luxes. Here it is quite easy to say that it is bright outside. However, if we measure a workspace to have 110 luxes, the room is still brightly illuminated. That doesn't sound very meaningful to a man. Hence, the borderline cases are difficult to handle.

The problem exists in the binary logic of the computer. Outdoor light level can be either dark or bright. Fuzzy logic presents a solution called multi-value logic. Using multi-value logic illumination level can be dark and bright at the same time, that is more than two truth-values exist. Here, it possible for illumination level to be at the same time much bright but little dark. There is no need to define exact bounds for continuous values and the different regions of truth can overlap each other. [8]

Linguistic variables are used in fuzzy systems as a method for performing calculations. The values of linguistic variables can be presented using membership functions that define the degree of membership in real input or output spaces. [8] Figure 2 demonstrates how the linguistic variable 'illuminance' is defined with values 'dark', 'normal' and 'bright'. For example, with a real input value of 150 from a light sensor illuminance is characterized to be dark in degree of 0, normal in degree of 0.8 and bright in degree of 0.2.

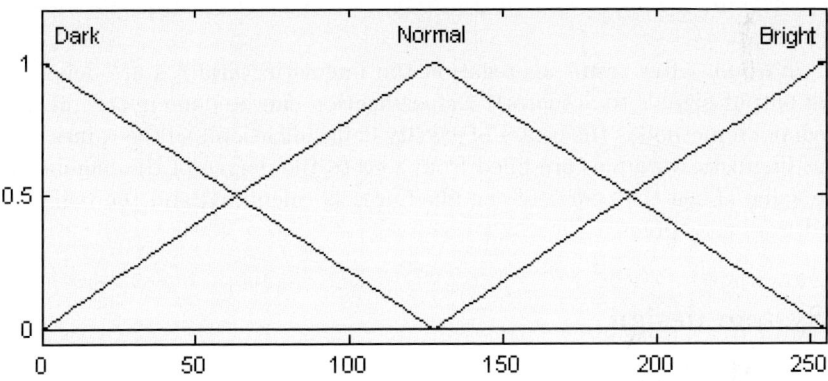

Fig. 2. Linguistic variable 'illuminance' defined with three membership functions

Fuzzy control Fuzzy control systems have many abilities that conventional control systems don't possess because of their multi-value logic. Fuzzy control includes three major steps: fuzzification, fuzzy inference and defuzzification. [8]

Fuzzification In order to be able to do fuzzy inference the real measurement values must be fuzzified. Fuzzification is performed using membership functions that define the input spaces and the values' degrees of membership for each variable separately. During fuzzification, every value of a linguistic variable receives a degree of membership based on the definition of the membership function and on the real measurement. An example of this was already presented with the linguistic variable 'illuminance' in the last chapter.

Fuzzy inference Fuzzy systems utilize a relatively simple rule table that represents the behavior of the whole system. The rules are of 'if – then' type. In the 'if' part the inputs' and in the 'then' part the outputs' linguistic variables' values are defined. 'If' part determines whether the rule is or is not valid in the current situation. 'Then' part is used to define the states of the outputs.

All the fuzzified input values must be aggregated to achieve a complete degree of truth to a rule. The aggregation is usually done using a minimum operator that takes the smallest degree of membership of the values of the input variables.

Composition follows next from the input aggregation. In the composition step the aggregated degree of truth of the 'if' part is multiplied by a weighing factor to get a degree of support (DoS) for the whole rule. Weighing factor or weight is associated with each rule and describes the significance of the rule. The weighing factor is usually defined to be in the interval [0, 1].

Since many of the rules can be true at the same time to a different degree, the result must be aggregated for each output variable's value separately. This is usually done by selecting the biggest result after the composition step controlling the output's value. This value determines the linguistic variables' output's degree of membership.

Defuzzification After result aggregation the linguistic variables are defuzzified to real output signals to actuators. Defuzzification can be done in several ways. One common method is the center of gravity defuzzification. All the values of the output linguistic variables are filled from zero to the degree of the membership of the value. Then the center of the filled area is calculated and the real result is read from that point.

3   System design

3.1   Fuzzy variables

The fuzzy control system uses seven linguistic input variables. The main input variables are 'outdoor lighting level', 'person activity' and 'time'. In addition to these, the states of the two outputs and their corresponding override flags are considered as inputs. The two linguistic output variables used are 'ceiling lighting power' and 'Venetian blinds position'.

Inputs The operation of a fuzzy control system is based on context recognition. Only a few sensors are used to recognize contexts in the home environment. Many different types of sensors could be used, but we prefer to measure variables that directly relate to the use of lighting in a home. Measuring only a few variables makes also the implementation of the system simpler. The sensors used are person activity and outdoor lighting level.

During the design of the lighting control system we saw a need for the system to behave differently at different times of the day. Using time as an input the system is able to react differently in the morning and in the evening while the other conditions can be closely the same defined by the other two sensors.

Outdoor lighting level The system measures outdoor lighting level constantly to be able, for example, to close the Venetian blinds when it gets dark outside. We have presupposed that the outdoor lighting level affects the use of Venetian blinds and ceiling lights that are used as outputs. The outdoor lighting level sensor gives a real measurement value between 0 and 255. This value is fuzzified to a linguistic variable using similar membership functions as shown in figure 2. The membership functions overlap each other so that a softer control in achieved.

Person activity It is essential to know whether the inhabitant is in the controlled space. This is because we see that the control system must act differently when a person is present and when he is not. A person activity sensor is used to give out binary information. The sensor gives a real output value of 0 or 255. This value is fuzzified to two different values of the linguistic variable 'absent' and 'in place'. Using membership functions shown in figure 3 it can be seen, that only one membership function can receive a membership degree of one at a time.

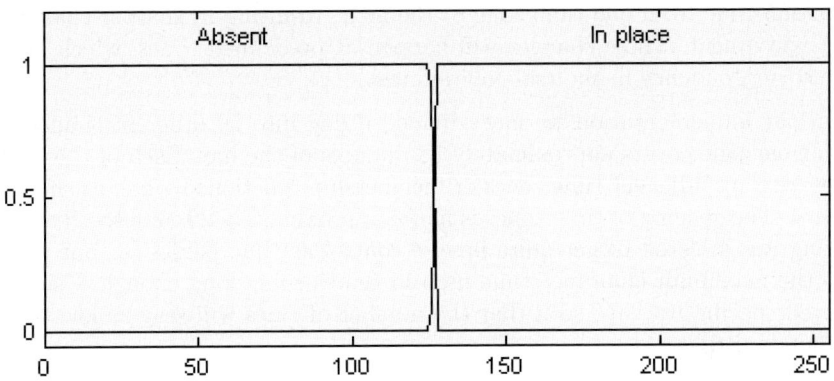

Fig. 3. Two membership functions of the linguistic variable 'person activity'

Time The system needs to be able to react differently to same conditions at different times of day. For example, an inhabitant may want to keep Venetian blinds closed in the morning and have them open in the evening. In this case, the measured conditions by the outdoor lighting and person activity sensors might be close to the same as in the morning. If time is not kept as an input to the system, the system cannot differentiate between the morning and the evening. Consequently time is an essential input of the fuzzy control system.

The system does not use an accurate clock with even a minute precision. Instead, a day has been divided to multiple time zones, which all cover several minutes of time. By using time zones instead of minutes, the amount of rules can be kept remarkably lower. If a minute scale should be used, there would be many rules for each minute. The usage of time zones also benefits the learning process. Long-time transient conditions that last for several minutes can easily be ignored, if a time zone is many times wider than the maximum ignorance time wanted in learning process.

There is no exact limit for the minimum number or width of time zones. However, the system's control time response is affected greatly, if a time zone is many hours in width. That happens, because within a single time zone only a limited set of rules can be effective. All of these rules must have the currently active time zone defined on the input side of the rule. These rules also remain effective throughout the time zone, if no new rules are learned.

It can be seen, that the optimal amount of overlap of adjacent time zones is one half. If the adjacent membership functions overlap each other by more than a half, the control accuracy remains still quite the same, if the width of a time zone still remains the same. However, more rules that have more closely the same outputs will generate to the rule base during learning as more than two membership functions overlap each other. In contrast, if the adjacent membership functions overlap each other by less than a half, there will be shorter transition time from one time zone to the next, resulting in sharper changes in the environment. These changes will happen at predefined times, which do not have correspondence in the real environment.

In our implementation we have divided a day into 50 different time zones. Each time zone covers approximately 58 minutes of the day. Each of these time zones overlaps adjacent time zones or membership functions by half as shown in figure 4. The spacing of time zones is hence approximately 29 minutes. The used spacing was selected to get quite precise control as time passes by, but also to keep the maximum ignorance time used in the learning long enough. Using the selected spacing we have seen that the number of rules will stay as low as in a few hundred rules.

The system receives the time as an ordinary input from the server's system clock. The time is represented in minutes (0 to 1440) from the beginning of the day. A problem arises when time passes midnight and the real time input value changes from 1440 to 0. Rules having time defined by the first and the last membership functions may have different outputs. This can cause the outputs to suddenly change at midnight, when the effective rules change. A smooth transition is required at midnight as it is on other times of the day.

Since time's continuity can be visualized with a circle, but the real input range of the linguistic variable 'time' is represented with a line, time must be artificially made continuous. To accomplish this, one extra membership function is presented. This extra membership function is inserted in the beginning of the real time scale and the other membership functions are moved 28 minutes further. Hence, both the first and the last membership functions reside half out of the used time scale. If the rules including the first and the last membership functions have same outputs, a smooth transition is achieved when time passes midnight. Using this method, only 50 membership functions actually can be thought to reside in the used time scale and the time is handled as continuous.

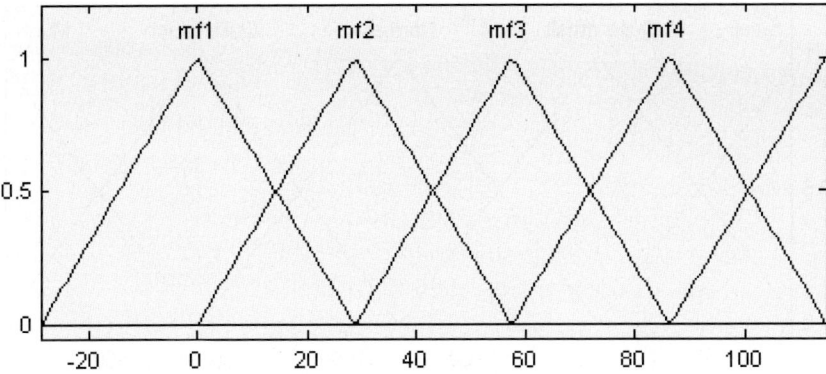

Fig. 4. The first four membership functions of the linguistic variable 'time'. The real time is represented in minutes from the beginning of the day.

Override flags The fuzzy control system must know if the output devices are overridden, in order to able to swap to event based control. The home controller keeps record on the user overrides and gives out the real values to fuzzy control system. The state of the overrides is represented with linguistic variables 'ceiling lighting override flag' and 'Venetian blinds override flag'. Both variables' values are 'off' and 'on' and are determined by similar shaped membership functions as shown in figure 3. The first membership function defines the 'off' state and the second membership function the 'on' state.

Actuators as inputs The states of the actuators are used as inputs to enhance the accuracy of the context recognition when event based control is used. The linguistic variables of these inputs are named with the same names as used with the outputs. The input linguistic variables utilize exactly the same membership functions as the output linguistic variables use.

Outputs Two different kinds of actuators are used to change the lighting environment in a home. The ceiling lights provide artificial light from above and Venetian blinds adjust the amount of light coming in through windows.

Ceiling lights Ceiling lights utilize a linguistic variable 'ceiling lighting power'. The variable has five different linguistic values as shown in figure 5. The membership functions of these values are laid evenly and overlap each other. The overlap makes a soft control more achievable. During defuzzification, the linguistic values are converted to a real value using center of gravity method. This real control value range of ceiling lights is defined to be 0 to 255. However, larger scale is used to set the 'small' and the 'much' membership functions enough out from the used scale, to achieve real outputs values of 0 or 255 using center of gravity method for result aggregation. If a real value outside the used scale is received from defuzzification, it is limited to the scale used.

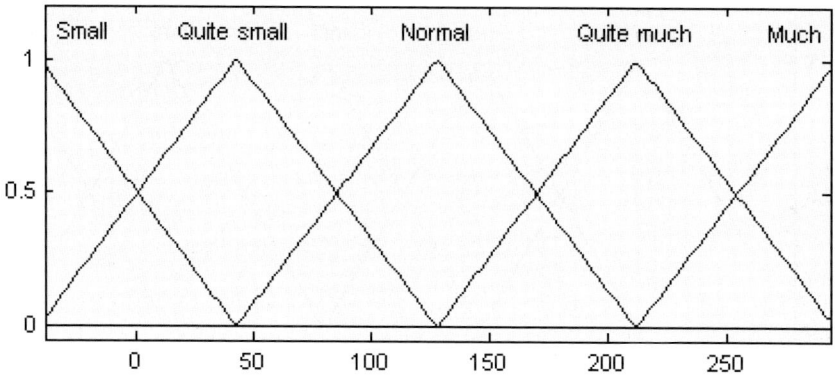

Fig. 5. The membership functions of the linguistic variable 'ceiling lighting power'

Venetian blinds The position of the Venetian blinds is defined in the fuzzy control with a linguistic variable 'Venetian blinds position'. The variable has five different values: 'closed down', 'down', 'center', 'up' and 'closed up'. All of these values have membership functions, which are similar to membership functions shown in figure 5. The real scale used for controlling the blinds is also from 0 to 255. A zero marks the 'closed down' position and 255 the 'closed up' position. For same reasons as described above, a larger real scale is used with Venetian blinds as well as with ceiling lighting.

3.2   Fuzzy control

The fuzzy control system monitors the context of the home with input devices and changes the environment using its actuators according to learned rules. Inhabitants don't need to interfere with the control system at all, but can override the actuators if needed. Two control modes, autonomous control and event-based control, are provided to make the system function better in different situations.

Conventional switches on the walls or other user interfaces let the user define an exact state for the actuator. If an actuator is manually adjusted, the control of the actuator is taken away from the fuzzy control system and the user is given a direct control over that device. At the same time, autonomous control is halted and event-based control takes charge of all other devices that are not overridden.

Autonomous control can be resumed by inactivating overrides. A special button for this use is provided to inhabitants. No automatic method to return to autonomous control is provided, because the user may want to teach the house even while he is no longer present.

Autonomous control In autonomous control mode the system is totally self-ruling and independent. The user does not need to concentrate on controlling the home, for the home adapts to the changes observed. The context of the home is analyzed at all times and the actuators are proactively adjusted when a change in the context is recognized.

Inference The problem solving or inference between input and output variables in the system is based on a rule table. Each rule has its own row in the table. The columns represent the values of the linguistic variables of inputs and outputs. Each rule defines a certain context with its inputs and the corresponding outputs define the states of the actuators.

In fuzzy inference, rules that depict the current situation, that is have linguistically same fuzzy input values as currently measured, receive a DoS value over zero. Here minimum operator is used for input aggregation and maximum operator for the composition step. All rows that get a DoS value above zero define the linguistic output values targeted. If no rule gets a DoS value over zero, the actuators positions are not altered.

An example of a rule base with three rules is shown in table 1. The first value or membership function of a linguistic variable is marked with one, the second with number two and so on. The first two rows show an example of rows used for autonomous control. The override rule type in the last row is used in event-based control.

Table 1. An example of a rule table

Linguistic variable / Rule type	Inputs								Outputs	
	Ceiling lighting override flag	Ceiling lighting power	Venetian blinds override flag	Venetian blinds position	Room lighting level	Outdoor lighting level	Person activity	Time	Ceiling lighting power	Venetian blinds position
Autonomous	1	0	1	0	3	3	1	12	2	3
Autonomous	1	0	1	0	2	1	2	40	5	1
Override	1	0	2	5	3	2	2	0	4	0

Table 2 shows all the possible types of rules used and the possible values in the rule table with the used rules. In autonomous control, the override flags of outputs on the input side are defined to be off, marked with number one. The output states on the input side are marked with zeros, so that the state of an output is ignored during the input aggregation. All the other values of the variables can be anything in the range of the used membership functions count. The override type rules used in event-based control are covered in the next chapter.

Table 2. Rule base definition with all possible types of rules

Linguistic variable / Rule type	Inputs								Outputs	
	Ceiling lighting override flag	Ceiling lighting power	Venetian blinds override flag	Venetian blinds position	Room lighting level	Outdoor lighting level	Person activity	Time	Ceiling lighting power	Venetian blinds position
Autonomous	1	0	1	0					Any	
Override	2	1-5	1	0	Any				0	1-5
Override	1	0	2	1-5					1-5	0
Not possible	2	0	2	0					Any	

Fuzzy control process The fuzzy control process runs continuously. The home controller enquires sensors every second and passes the information to the fuzzy control system if any of the input variables change. The measurements are fuzzified, fuzzy outputs are calculated in fuzzy inference and then defuzzified using the center of gravity method into real control signals. The real output values are then forwarded to the home controller, which sets the actuators to the positions wanted. If a user generates an event by overriding an actuator, all inputs are immediately measured and passed to the fuzzy control process.

Event based control To achieve a more proactive and context sensitive control system, we propose that in addition to autonomous control the actuators should also be controlled as they are manually being adjusted. For example, as a user manually overrides autonomous control and closes the Venetian blinds, the system can adjust the ceiling lights to another power setting learned.

The context is sensed at the time of an event also with the state where the actuator was displaced and with the other input parameters as well. However, time is excluded, because we see that the learning process of these event based rules would take too much time, if separate rules for each time zone ought to be learned. The control system couldn't do anything in case of an event, if the time zone was wrong.

To enable these proactive actions based on user adjustments, a class of override rules is introduced as shown in tables 1 and 2. Contrary to autonomous rules, these event-based rules have one or more override flags lifted up. However, not all override flags can be up in a rule at the same time. The rules with all override flags lifted up would be useless, because the fuzzy control system couldn't control the actuators in any case.

These override rules tell the fuzzy control system to control all the other outputs that are not overridden based on the current situation or context. During fuzzy inference, the rules that depict the current environment become effective and the outputs are changed in a normal fashion. The value of the corresponding linguistic variable of the manually adjusted actuator is marked in the rule base with a zero, to show that the actuator will not be adjusted.

3.3   Learning process

The fuzzy control system can learn its rule table without prior knowledge and does not need any training prior to use. It can add and remove rules and modify existing ones based on the learned information. With this versatile learning ability, a fuzzy control system can become totally unnoticeable after its initialization.

Learning process is based on monitoring the context in the home. Fuzzy control system monitors input and output devices, so it is always aware of the state of the home. Teaching is done in four steps, which are gathering of data, fuzzification of data, filtering and updating the rule base. These steps and the conncetion between the home controller and the learning process are shown in figure 6. Teaching is controlled by timers that define how often these steps occur.

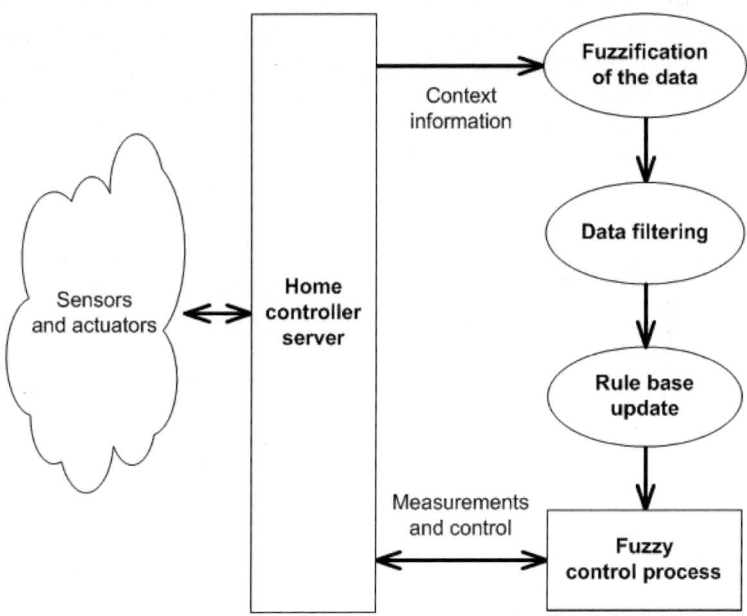

Fig. 6. The learning process as a part of the system structure

Saving context information Gathering the data is a continuous process. The purpose of this step is to get enough data of users actions so that routines become clear. As mentioned, the fuzzy control system monitors both the input and the output devices. It writes their current values periodically to storage. A timer controls this process. The interval of the timer therefore defines the amount of data gathered. Because this data is filtered at later stages, this interval does not really define what the system will learn. Instead, it defines the sampling period and the duration of which the system does not have any information.

If data is written once a minute, the system does not know what happened during that minute. User may have changed some output to some other value and back, and the system has no idea what happened. Therefore this writing interval should not be very long. On the other hand, there is no use to write information for example once per second. The conditions of the home do not change that often, even when user controls it, and most of the information would be filtered out anyway. We came to a conclusion that one minute was a reasonable timer interval for writing data. With that sampling rate the system gets enough data to process, and the system is not needlessly encumbered by collecting too much data that is not needed in the first place.

Fuzzifying the data Processing the data starts with fuzzification. Both the inputs and the outputs are read from their storage and fuzzified to a value representing their membership function with the greatest degree of membership. The value of this linguistic variable is then stored in order to be used in the learning process. The time input variable is treated slightly differently. Instead of choosing the membership function with the greatest degree of membership, system picks all membership functions whose degree of membership exceeds a given threshold. All these time values are then used in the learning process. This way the system learns also a little for times that are adjacent to the current time. This smoothens the transitions from one time membership function to another. In addition, it is useful in early stages of teaching when there are only a few or no rules in rule base. When the next time zone is used as well as the current one, the system always has at least one rule to use when time advances to the next zone.

Filtering the data When the data is fuzzified, it is filtered. System searches the most common combination of inputs and outputs from each data batch, but disregards the time input values. All other combinations than the most common one are ignored. Time input is ignored at this moment so that every situation under the measurement time can be compared to each other regardless of the time zone. The purpose of this filtering is to ignore all transient states and discover the dominant conditions for that time period. It also removes the element of chance that comes from sampling.

Here the size of the batch is important. It must not be longer than one membership function of the time input variable, because then it would be possible that system would not generate rules for some membership functions. This sets the upper limit, which is 58 minutes. The teaching interval also defines the maximum ignorance time. That is the shortest time of constant conditions that is guaranteed to be taught. This time is same as the teaching interval if the interval is an odd number of minutes. With an even number of minutes this time is one minute less than the teaching interval.

We chose to use the teaching interval of 15 minutes. This sets the maximum ignorance time to 15 minutes, so the system guarantees to teach all conditions that last at least that long. Conditions that do not last that long are most likely transients and not relevant to the system. When the most common combination of the inputs and the outputs is found, the system finds all times from the data batch that this combination has occurred. This way the input and the output pairs are completed. These combinations are then edited into the rule base.

Updating the rule base The rule base is edited in three ways. The rules are added, possibly removed, and their weighing factors are edited. The rule base is searched for input combinations that were found in the previous step. If the input combination is not found, then the corresponding rule is added to the rule base with a small initial weighing factor. If one or more input combinations are found however, their output combinations are then compared to the new rule. If a rule has the same output combination as the new rule, its weighing factor is increased and so that rule becomes more dominant. On the other hand, if the output combinations differ, the weighing factor is decreased respectively. If the weighing factor becomes zero, the rule is removed from the rule base. The amount of increase is constant, which is designed to take the weighing factor from zero to one in approximately two days, assuming constant conditions. Reasoning behind the two-day period is that the constant conditions observed during one day might be an exception, but two consecutive days of the same conditions should have an impact on the system behaviour.

Teaching override rules In teaching, the overrides are managed in two ways. The overrides are the mechanism used to tell the system what it should learn. Therefore the normal rules used in the autonomous mode must always be taught. This means that even when one override for some actuator is on, the normal autonomous control is taught as if it was not. These rules then determine how the system behaves when it is in the autonomous mode.

The override rules, which define the event-based actions, are learned in a normal fashion, by adding rules and increasing and decreasing the weighing factors. However, there is one big difference in handling the override rules: they are time-independent. In practise these rules have a zero in their time input field and therefore they can be active no matter what the time is.

4   Discussion

The system was tested in a smart home described above. Users could use all methods for controlling the apartment that were available already before this study, so no new user interfaces were necessary. Testing gave us valuable feedback that was not easy to obtain through the simulations. Some of the enhancements were implemented as the work progressed, but most are to be addressed to in the next version of the fuzzy control system.

4.1   Acceptance

Both the simulations and the testing clearly showed that a fuzzy control system is very well suited for proactive control. The system is capable of learning through observing the users' actions, and it is quick to anticipate the users' routines. After the initialization, it takes only a few days to learn enough rules that the need for user intervention decreases dramatically. If routines are changed, it takes only a couple of days to consolidate new rules for that routine and get rid of the old ones.

Since inhabitants' needs are not constant from day to day, it is inevitable that from time to time the needs will be different from what the fuzzy system determines. However, we found out that the decisions of the fuzzy system do not need to correspond exactly with what the user is planning to do. We see that most of the time we do not have very strict demands for how our lighting should be adjusted. Since we only notice when the lighting is clearly wrong, the anticipation of the process is much easier. Therefore it suffices that the proactive actions take the environment close enough to the wanted conditions.

4.2   Managing the time

The time handling proved to be a quite important part of the system operation. Three significant time related parameters were identified to have a great influence on the behaviour of the system. These parameters are the input variable 'time' and its membership functions, the data gathering interval and the teaching interval. They all are dependent from each other and a careful cross evaluation is needed while selecting them. Especially the behaviour of the learning process changes with the parameter modifications.

The dominating parameter that sets the limit to other parameters is the input variable 'time' and its membership functions. The width of the membership functions defines the upper limit for the number of membership functions, because it is not practical to have membership functions that almost completely overlap each other. The number of membership functions has a significant effect on the control accuracy. A large number of membership functions mean a more accurate control, but it forces the teaching interval to be shorter, as the teaching interval must not be any longer than the duration defined by the membership function. A shorter teaching interval also means that shorter lasting conditions are taught to the system. This is not desirable, since transients should not be learned. The teaching interval must therefore be selected so that the transient conditions are filtered out. Finally, the teaching interval sets the upper limit to the data gathering interval. The data gathering interval must clearly be much shorter than the teaching interval. Otherwise the filtering becomes pointless.

As the system is designed for a long-term control it does not have very strict requirements for the time parameters. It is practically irrelevant whether there are 50 time zones rather than 49. Due to a continuous nature of these parameters it is also difficult to pinpoint any specific optimal value for them. Therefore the initial values of these parameters were selected with an educated guess. Naturally the parameters were trimmed during the simulations until we reached the current values and concluded that they were working well. They are by no means the only suitable values, but we found that they are feasible for this prototype. In the future a method for initializing these parameters should be developed.

4.3   Future work

During the research we found out some difficulties that the system had. One such problem was the behaviour of the event-based control. It was meant to work as a means to create event-based chains of events, but we found out it did not have enough information about the context. When every user override action created an override rule, the system could not distinguish if the adjustment had anything to do with the other actuators. Based on the small number of sensors used it is very hard to recognize the context and reason why a user made that change. This added to the fact that as the event-based control is not time-dependent the user overriding actions often caused automatic control on the other actuators. That appeared to the user as an unexpected and random behaviour. We found out that observing chains of events does not fit well to fuzzy systems, and therefore it is not practical to create an event-based system using fuzzy control. Instead, a method of sequential pattern mining first introduced in [11] and moreover utilized in [12] could be more efficient in discovering these sequences.

We also came up with another problem with the override rules. The issue was that the override rules paralysed the autonomous control process. Since every user override action was treated as an event that activated some override rules, it meant that all actions caused the normal control process to stop, even when no suitable override rules were present. It would have been better if overriding one actuator would only stop autonomous control for that single actuator and leave the rest as they were. This problem should be solved in the future versions of the system.

At the beginning of the study we considered to use an indoor lighting level sensor in the apartment as an input device. The goal was to enable us to keep lighting level inside the apartment at a constant level even when the lighting level outside would change over time. However, the simulations illustrated that it was a bad idea to create a feedback like this into the fuzzy system. If a rule has an input that is affected by the outputs of the rule and the rule becomes effective, the system ends up in a situation where the outputs of the rule cause it to be instantly made ineffective. With two or more rules of this kind this can lead to oscillation between the rules. Since the outputs may swing drastically or the rules can make themselves ineffective, the effect cannot be accepted. Therefore the indoor lighting level sensor was dropped out at early stages of this study. However, a new method for including the indoor lighting level sensor should be researched.

Some difficulties arose with the learning when the user was absent. Since overrides are on indefinitely and the system learns continuously, a user can easily ignore the fact that when he leaves the room, the learning does not stop. Instead the system learns from whatever conditions the user left the room with. This might not be a problem, but in practise it means that every once in a while the system learns something that is not desired. Because of the nature of the learning, these rules are then strengthened if the user does not actively intervene with the overrides. Our objective was that the user should need to be aware of the operation of the system as little as possible, so this is not desirable. It became clear that handling situations, where the user is absent, must be reconsidered in the future versions of this system.

The large number of time zones is good for handling the time fairly accurately, but it also creates a challenge for the learning process. Lots of time zones produce a large number of input combinations, which means that it takes a long time to learn the rules for each input combination. Especially at the early stages of learning it is quite common that no applicable rule is found. If an effective rule cannot be found, then no automatic adjustments can be made and the system is not very useful. When the system starts learning without prior knowledge, it is important to generate quickly enough rules to function properly. Therefore we seek to find a solution, which minimizes these no-rule situations.

The currently used method for editing the weighing factors must be enhanced. Since humans' routines are quite imprecise, the rules get both strengthened and weakened by a constant value at a regular basis. The current method is quite functional, but we have seen that it leads the system to situation where the rule base has a lot of medium strength rules that try to control the lighting to different directions. In practice, this can be seen as lots of loose adjustments near the center of the real control range of the actuators. From the users point of view this is not very useful. Hence, we must design a better, nonlinear algorithm for editing the weighing factors.

5   Conclusion

Already at the beginning of the research we saw a fuzzy control system to be an interesting tool in order to reach the objectives. The simulations were promising and an actual working system was implemented for the smart home laboratory. Some user tests were carried out, which highlighted many of the development areas in the system. The event-based control mode was found inadequate and the times when the user is absent problematic. However, the basic system functioned as planned and many good results were obtained. Particularly the learning method used proved to be successful.

In conclusion, we found that the basic fuzzy control system structure is a suitable method. In the lighting control purposes the developed system has been seen to perform quite well and it is plausible that the basic structure could be brought to use on other home control systems as well. Nevertheless, it is clear that much additional work will be required before such a control system will be ready to be taken into extensive use.

References

1. Mäntyjärvi, J., Seppänen, T. Adapting applications in handheld devices using fuzzy context information, Interacting with Computers, vol. 15, issue 4, p. 521-538, August 2003
2. Pirttikangas, S., Routine Learning: from Reactive to Proactive Environments, University of Oulu, Faculty of Technology, 2004
3. Tennenhouse D., Proactive Computing, Communications of the ACM, May 2000, vol. 43, no. 5, pp. 43-50
4. Byun, H. E., Cheverst, K. Supporting proactive "intelligent" behaviour: the problem of uncertainty, Proc. Workshop on User Modelling for Ubiquitous Computing, User Modeling 2003
5. Mozer, M.C. Intelligent Systems and Their Applications, IEEE, vol. 2, no. 2, March/April, p. 11-13, 1999
6. Buckley J. J., Hayashi Y. & Czogala E. On the equivalence of neural networks and fuzzy expert systems, Proc. IJCNN-92, Baltimore, vol. 2, p. 691-695, 1992
7. Kaila, L., Vainio, A.-M., Vanhala, J., Connecting the smart home, IASTED, Networks and Communication Systems, April 18-20, 2005, pp. 445-450
8. Wang, L. X., A course in fuzzy systems and control, Prentice Hall PTR, 1997
9. Kaila, L., The Intelligent home of the future. Master of Science Thesis, Tampere University of Technology, Institute of Electronics, 2001, 93 p. (in Finnish)
10. Vainio, A.-M., Control system for Intelligent Home Environment, Master of Science Thesis, Tampere University of Technology, Institute of Software Systems, 2006, 71 p. (in Finnish)
11. Agrawal, R., Srikant, R., Mining Sequential Patterns, ICDE '95: Proceedings of the Eleventh International Conference on Data Engineering, IEEE Computer Society, Washington, DC, USA, pp. 3-14, 1995
12. Guralnik, V., Haigh, K. Z., Learning Models of Human Behaviour with Sequential Patterns, Proceedings of the AAAI-02 workshop "Automation as Caregiver", pp. 24-30, 2002

Protocol for a truly distributed coordination among agents in competitive survival video-games

Julio Cano and Javier Carbó

Applied Artificial Intelligent Group
Carlos III University of Madrid
Spain
{jcano,jcarbo}@inf.uc3m.es

Abstract. Competition games are dynamic and distributed scenarios where agent technology is often applied. In this context, agents form collaborative coalitions that compete for a goal. Inside such type of coalitions of equals, we cannot centralize coordination on a single agent nor allocate tasks on a given agent by default. A protocol is proposed here to work in such conditions. This protocol is similar to a decentralized Contract Net, but initiator agent does not centralize agent task allocation. This problem is solved through a global system rank that selects the most suited agents for the task. This interaction protocol has been implemented and tested under different simulated conditions, showing a high level of success.

1 Introduction

In recent years, there has been an increasing interest in extending the use of Internet. With this intention, automation and delegation is desirable to exploit the possibilities of spanning geographical, cultural and political boundaries. It can be achieved through the use of autonomous programs often called 'agents'.

From the very different goals that agents try to accomplish in electronic environments, this research is interested just in how they coordinate their efforts towards a shared goal. Many agent coordination protocols have already been proposed for general purpose like TAEMS [11] and GPGP [1]. But their coordination is based on specialized agents like matchmakers, brokers, etc, or like Contract Net in witch contractor agent centralizes the task allocation.

Since we intend to achieve coordination in a coalition of agents that play no special role of coordination (a society of equals) a new interaction protocol is required.

The proposed protocol is mainly a variation of Contract Net, but modified according to restrictions and conditions of a specific environment (detailed in the next section). These restrictions try to describe most video games environments where several human and/or computerized players (agents) interact and play the game.

The agents that participate in the proposed protocol are supposed to be basically situated agents, but with the ability to communicate with others through direct messages. So they can not be considered as a purely Situated MultiAgent System. The terms: capabilities, characteristics and situation are used indifferently along this paper, indicating whole agent situation, when applied to agents. They could reference the agent position in a map, availability to accomplish a given task, quantity of knowledge the agent has, etc. These agent characteristics are supposed to change dynamically along the time.

The next section describes restrictions that apply to the problem. Section 3 enumerates different approaches to solve the problem and why these approaches don't resolve completely the problem. In section 4 a BDI model is introduced so that agents can implement this protocol. In section 5 and 6 the protocol is described and analyzed. Possible modifications are proposed in section 7 and section 8 concludes.

2   Problem description and restrictions

Most competitive videogames can be modelled as distributed and highly dynamic environments. Some of the characteristics that usually describe a video game environment are as follow:

- Dynamicity:
  Agents situation changes constantly. That makes almost useless to advertise agent services or characteristics when the agent enters into the system, because these will change along the time. The characteristics or situation of the agent needs to be checked every time a request is made or a goal is marked to be accomplished, and right in that moment, so that the best agent can be selected to do the task. As agent situation or characteristics change so dynamically and constantly along the time it results useless to publish, store and centralize them like their position in a map.
- Agents falling (dying):
  Although the kind of services provided by an agent could be published and registered or concentrated in specialized agents acting as central entities like matchmakers, brokers, etc., these services will depend on agent situation at every moment. And therefore the central agent should be asking every agent about its situation before selecting one of them for a task.
  Moreover we are assuming a completely distributed environment in which only agents that are able to interact with other agents or the environment itself are represented. So this kind of middleware agents should be avoided. Another main reason to avoid concentration of information on a single specialized agent is that in competitive multiagent systems (such as video games), agents can enter, exit the system or even fall (being eliminated) at any time, losing all that information.
  All these reasons lead to a distributed system of agents with minimum hierarchical organization. Then, distributed coordination protocols that avoid centralization become really relevant.

– Teams (or coalitions) setup:
  In distributed agent systems such as described here teams setup is an important issue. Although out goal is not to solve this problem, this interaction protocol could be used to select team components individually or by sending a special kind of multiple request and then form the team. Communications security is not considered in this paper, so communications among team members in competitive games are supposed to be separated so that enemies can not hear team or broadcast messages.
– Communications load:
  One of the biggest problems in distributed systems is communications overload due to the quantity of information that is required to be exchanged. This proposal does not come to solve this problem as the general usage of this protocol still requires a large number of messages sent in the system for an agent or a group of agents (the best suited) to be chosen for a task allocation. Given the conditions described above these messages are needed if the agent that centralizes, processes all the information and makes the choice fails to complete the process. This work is repeated so many times as agents intend to accomplish the task; since it is currently replicated by every one of these agents comparing themselves to the others.
– Availability (Dynamism):
  Sometimes, in competitive distributed systems, accomplish a given goal (petition) is essential to win (or lose). If the petition sender agent or any other central agent fails or dies, then the allocated task will not be completed and the corresponding goal might never be reached. This is a typical situation in video games in which a defender agent can ask for support when the team base is attacked. If a Contract Net were used and the defender was killed in the interaction process, the supporter could never be selected and therefore the base would be left undefended as shown in Figure 1. This is one of the main reasons this kind of coordination protocol is needed.
– Benevolence:
  In a cooperative environment, decisions are made based on benevolence of the rest of the team agents. In this proposal agents' benevolence is supposed. If there is a common goal then benevolence will be needed for team work. If agents lie about their capabilities or situation then a wrong selection will be made. Several other architectures and protocols have the same problem, which can be treated with different trust models like such as [2], etc. These techniques are not discussed in this paper.

3   Some previous coordination protocols

There are several protocols dealing with the coordination problem. But must of them result useless or very hard to be effective on some truly dynamic or risky environments. Some of the most relevant protocols are outlined in this section to show the differences with the proposed protocol.

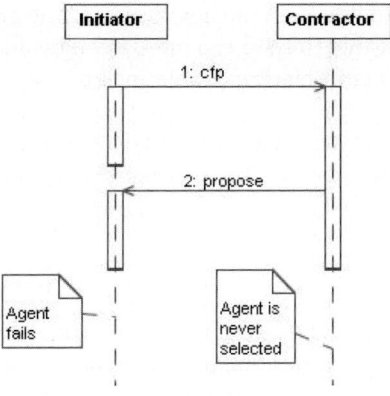

Fig. 1. Example of agent failure

3.1   RETSINA

RETSINA [11] is a distributed multiagent system that uses a hierarchical organization divided in three layers. The first layer is constituted by interface agents, dealing with users. The second one is formed by task agents receiving requests from interface agents, splitting them in subtasks and allocating them. Finally information agents receive requests from task agents. Once data are retrieved by information agents it is sent back being processed until interface level.

Task agents use HTN (Hierarchical Task Networks) for their organization, tasks and actions scheduling. Different kind of plans libraries like general or domain specific are used for that. This means that task agents' hierarchy will depend on plan libraries and it will be mainly static. If a few task agents become out of order some functions of the information system will not be available. In a different environment like a competitive video game it could make some basic capabilities of the team to not be available. The team would not can to win the game. Task allocation is made by matchmaking in which every agent that provides a service must be registered. These matchmaking agents are supposed to do not fail either, because this would mean that all the registered agents would not be available. And if agents are continuously going in and out of the system a lot of messages to register and unregister them would be exchanged.

So this architecture still lacks of enough dynamicity to provide reliability in a dynamic distributed and coordinated system like a video game.

3.2   GPGP

GPGP is very useful to schedule group tasks and to coordinate agents or different groups even in a monitored and synchronized way.

In [1] only the group leader sends commitment messages to other groups. If the group leader is not available then the next agent of the group in a predetermined hierarchy is the responsible to send the message. This hierarchy will accumulate several timeouts if agents in hierarchy fail, until message is sent from a group to another.

Even with proposed enhancements to GPGP, the quantity of communication messages and needed time can not be reduced. Commitment messages exchanged in a group are still of O(N2).

3.3   Contract Net

Contract Net is an extensively used interaction protocol. It has been adopted by FIPA [6]. But it can vary depending on implementation details.

It consists mainly in a contractor initiating the protocol dialog sending a Call For Proposals to the rest of participants in the dialog. These participants send their proposals back to the initiator. The initiator accepts or rejects proposals depending on his interests.

As can be seen all the selection process and information is concentrated in the initiator. The risk here will be to not complete the dialog if the initiator is eliminated of the system.

4   BDI model of the proposed agents

In this section a reasoning model based on BDI [10] paradigm is described for agents to participate in the coordination protocol. Only a partial model is given, so it does not include specific beliefs, desires and intentions an agent may need to do its work. Relevant elements to the coordination protocol are described next:
   Beliefs:

- Requests/Goals: The agent needs to keep a list with goals or requests received. These goals can be modelled in several ways depending on the way the services offered in the system are modelled. Basic elements to include in the goal specifications can be the next:
- Sender: The agent that publishes the goal.
- Ontology/Ambit: A context must be specified in which petition has a determined meaning. It can be represented by ontology or a working area or ambit. Generally this ambit will let us classify agents according to their characteristics or available capabilities.
- Action: The request itself specifies the concrete task to be accomplished. It will be interpreted depending on the previous ontology.
- Quantity: It could be included in the previous attribute. Represents the exact number of agents needed or recommended to complete the petition.
- Petition identification: Useful internally and in communications with other agents. Should allow a unique identification in the system. It could be based on the sender's system identification and a counter, supposing a unique identification for the agent.

- Delays/Deadlines: Waiting times associated to the task actions, like minimum time waited before responding to the petition or deadline to be accomplished.
- Restrictions: Generally related to request application, needed to discard agents that would not can to accomplish the task.
- Ranks: A global ranking is made in which every agent in the system knows his own position, respectively to every petition sent, indicating its adequateness to the petition requirements. So, a rank position must be associated to every petition in agent's beliefs list.
- Characteristics/Capabilities: These represent the rest of beliefs the agent has. These ones do not need to match capabilities specification o services this agent offers, but a complete or partial vision of these characteristics will be exchanged among agents so that they can compare themselves and determine their rank position.

Desires/Goals:
Agent's goals can be split in two kinds:

- Own goals: Agent will have his own goals so that he can work independently or autonomously. These goals are optional, making the agent to act only on demand.
- Foreign or Group goals: Agent can receive requests from other agents, creating new goals independently from owns to work in group or serve other agents.
  In case of not accepting external requests, the agent is supposed to be autonomous and will not work in group. So it will not use this kind of coordination protocol and does not need to adopt this formalization, at least as service provider. It still could send requests to the system and even receive responses in case that they are needed.
  One of the reasons of choosing BDI paradigm for the agent model is that it can deal easily with conflicting goals. In this case priority of own or external goals is determined by agent situation and planning.

Intentions/Plans:
There are two plans directly related to the protocol as defined here:

- Accept Petition: This plan must accept incoming requests to the agent, determine if these requests correspond to agent capabilities, assign a global rank value corresponding to such petition (initially 1), check out specified restrictions and act after indicated deadline if agent is in the needed rank.
- Accept Capability/Situation Descriptions: In parallel with the previous plan. After accepting a petition, a message with agent situation is sent to the rest of agents. So messages with characteristics of the rest of agents will be received. This plan compares information included in every message received to own characteristics to determine agent rank position.

5   The proposed Coordination Protocol

This protocol can be considered basically as a Contract Net without a contractor role. Contractor role is reduced just to send the petition. Actually contractor role is distributed and replicated at the rest of agents.

Noticing restrictions imposed to problem, the petition sender (contractor) can not assure to be there to process offers from the rest of agents. In fact a petition could be not sent by an agent itself but any other element in the system. Once

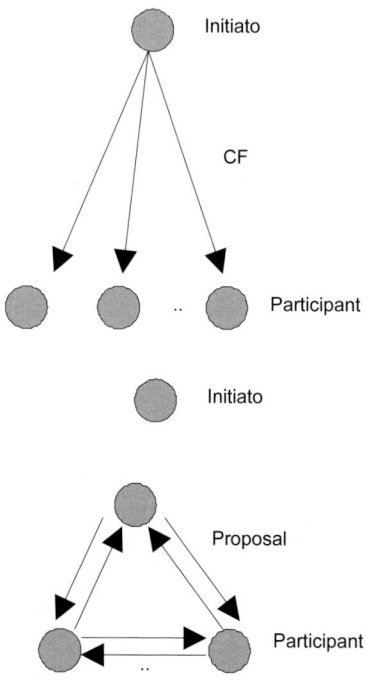

Fig. 2. Coordination protocol

the petition is sent, agents get into competition comparing their capabilities and situation among them to determine the optimum agent(s) to accomplish the solicited task in the given moment. In this competition a global ranking is created in which every agent will occupy a position depending on their characteristics or situation in that moment. A detailed description of the interaction protocol is as follows:

– An agent or element in the system sends a message to the other agents (a specific group of agents, like agent's team or known neighbours) with the description of the task to be accomplished. This description formulation is already given above.

— Every agent that receives the message checks if all the necessary restrictions are fulfilled to respond to petition. Restrictions can be of two kind:

— Own Restrictions: Those imposed by the agent itself to respond to the petition, like not being already working in another task, tasks incompatibilities, etc.

— Imposed Restrictions: Those described in the petition, like time to respond, maximum distance to a given target, etc.

— Once the agent checks that all restrictions are fulfilled, it initializes its global ranking position associated to the petition to 1, as it is going to participate in the selection.

— Every agent publishes its capabilities, characteristics or situation at that moment, sending it to the rest of agents. This message generally has to be sent to the rest of similar agents as the original receivers list is neither known by this agent nor which of them fulfil restrictions and will respond to the petition.

— Every agent waits a prefixed time, generally specified in the request, as a delay before starting the required action. During this time, messages specifying capabilities from other agents are processed. These characteristics are compared to own characteristics. This allows the modification of the global ranking position of the agent in the following way:

— In case that message characteristics are higher than own, value in global ranking is incremented. This means that if initially ranking position is 1 it is changed to 2. This actually represents a global ranking position decrement.

— In case of the other agent's characteristics being lower the message is just ignored and position at global ranking is not changed.

— In case that characteristics or situations are the same or equivalent a play-off is needed. As an initial proposal an identifiers comparison is suggested, so that identifier will determine priority in tie cases. Other play-off methods are encouraged given that unique identifiers represent to have a centralized access method to the system to ensure those identifiers are not repeated.

— Once specified delay time is over all messages with capabilities or situation at that moment from other agents must have been processed. So global rank belief must contain its final value. Then, ranking position is compared to the quantity of agents specified in the petition.

— If agent results to be among those with rank value lesser than or equal to that indicated in the petition, the specified goal at the petition is accepted by the agent as own, making the agent to start the corresponding task. In other case the agent has not been selected to do the task. Even then it could be useful to keep rank value associated to petition in beliefs list in case that other agents would not can to finish their task, so that next agents in ranking can be selected and start their work.

As can be seen, the optimum agents are selected for every petition at every moment. It is done without intermediaries, centralizing message exchange, information nor capabilities matching.

6   Analysis of the proposed protocol

Protocol described above represents a generic method applicable to all situations with restrictions imposed to the problem of finding optimum agent to accomplish a specific task in a given moment in a completely decentralized way.

Total number of exchanged messages is due to these strict restrictions and generalization. While time spent since petition is sent until a response is given is not necessarily longer than needed in Contract Net, as work is done in parallel. Total number of exchanged messages is O(N2), approximately N+A*N, being N the total number of agents and A the number of agents from N (A=N) that fulfil own and imposed restrictions. First N messages are requests sent from the sender and A*N are characteristics messages sent by competing agents for being selected.

Total time spent from request to response must be adjusted previously and specified in petition. At least a default value can be used for all requests. As in a Contract Net this delay time is needed so that all messages with characteristics information are sent and processed by every agent to determine ranking positions. If waiting time is not completed or messages are not completely processed agents will act according to not real rank values.

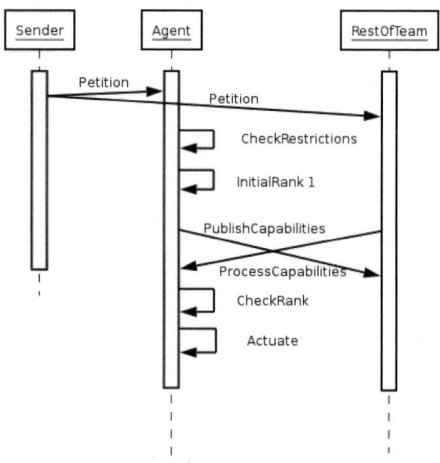

Fig. 3. Sequence diagram of an execution of the coordination protocol

Agents should not act before having received and processed all incoming messages from other agents or waited enough time. This time does not necessarily have to be greater than a Contract Net wait time.

This time is still much sorter than in synchronization mechanism proposed in [1] given that here there is no dependence of a leader and no timeouts are chained.

7   Possible optimizations of the proposed protocol

As stated above, protocol described here represents a general case with certain restrictions imposed. Depending on environment or system characteristics these restrictions can be relaxed and protocol modified or adapted adding enhancements to reduce the number of interchanged messages.

Here are described possible situations and modifications in the implementation of the protocol:

- Caching capabilities or characteristics of the rest of agents: Depending on how fast agent characteristics change along the time, messages sent by agents can include a time to life mark (time that the information is going to be considered valid). These characteristics can be included as agent beliefs. In case of receiving a new petition it will not be necessary to resend new messages with agent situation as this is still stored, until that agent situation has changed.
- Static Ranking: In case that situation varies slowly along the time a static ranking can be maintained. Every agent keeps referenced those preceding and next agents in the global ranking. If a new petition is received every agent will only exchange messages with those agents that are adjacent in the rank position. Once rank positions are adjusted, request can be answered.
- Utility function: Size of messages interchanged can be reduced significantly if a utility function is used. Given that every agent must use the same heuristics to compare characteristics of different agents a utility function can be used to send a utility value calculated from its characteristics.

  Even if agents' situation keeps quite stable along the time this method results useful to initiate a global optimum rank of agents depending on their capabilities. After that initiation phase, one of the simplifications described in this section can be used.

8   Simulation Tests of the proposed protocol

Different simulations have been created to test the protocol.

The first one simulates agents running across a room while requests are sent to ask for a certain number of agents to run to a given position. Task is accomplished while enough agents are available to complete the specified number. This is especially useful for future implementations of Unreal Tournament(c) Bots (Agents) team work.

The second test simulates an area watched by surveillance video cameras while objects are circulating. Video cameras use this protocol to control objects in the area as much time as possible. They do it by sending a petition to the rest of cameras to watch an object that has gone out of their vision range. Objects' control is successfully passed from one camera to the next. It is done while the next camera is free or does not lose control over other objects. Simulation works successfully independently of mobile cameras or even failing cameras in the area with available resources at every moment [7].

9   Conclusions

Video games are a very common testbed of agent systems, but current coordination protocols allocate tasks assuming a relatively stable environment. But survival competitive games include conditions such as the sudden fall/die of agents involved in the game. So classic coordination protocols seem to be not directly applicable to this kind of video games.

Interaction protocol proposed here comes to fulfil this gap, allowing requests to be responded under difficult conditions by all available agents in that moment. This proposal is made with the most difficult conditions and generalization in mind, resulting as a consequence of such strict requirements. If explicit implementations environments are not so strict, the protocol can be adapted as described in the previous section, reducing the communication load and even the delay to respond to requests.

This interaction protocol has been implemented and tested under different simulated ad-hoc experiments, working successfully. Next, we intend to test it on more real-time scenarios of video-games such as Unreal Tournament and other real-world coordination problem such as surveillance with cameras.

References

1. S. Abdallah, N. Darwish, O. Hegazy, Monitoring and Synchronization for Teamwork in GPGP.
   Proceedings of the 2002 ACM symposium on Applied computing, March 11-14, 2002, Madrid, Spain.
2. J. Carb, J. M., Molina, J. Dvila. "Trust Management through Fuzzy Reputation". International Journal of Cooperative Information Systems, vol. 12, num. 1, pp. 135-155 (March 2003).
3. W. Chen, K. Decker. Managing Multi-Agent Coordination, Planning, and Scheduling. AAMAS'04
4. K. Decker. "TAEMS: A Framework for Environment Centered Analysis & Design of Coordination Mechanisms." Funtadions of Distributed Artificial Intelligente, chapter 16.1996. pp. 429-448.
5. K. Decker, K. Sycara, M. Williamson, "Modeling Information Agents: Advertisements, Organizational Roles, and Dynamic Behavior," Working Notes of the (AAAI)-96 Workshop on Agent Modeling. 1996
6. FIPA Contract Net Interaction Protocol Specification. http://www.fipa.org/. 2001
7. J. Garca, J. Carb, J. Molina. "Agent-based Coordination of Cameras." International Journal of Computer Science & Applications. Special Issue on Applications of Software Agents in Engineering. Vol. 2, No. 1 (January 2005).
8. H. Muoz-Avila, T. Ficher. Strategic Planning for Unreal Tournament(c) Bots. Proceedings of AAAI-04 Workshop on Challenges on Game AI. 2004
9. S. Paurobally, J. Cunningham, N.R. Jennings. "Verifying the contract net protocol: a case study in interaction protocol and agent communication semantics." Proceedings of 2nd International Workshop on Logic and Communication in Multi-Agent Systems, pp. 98-117, Nancy, France 2004.

10. A. Rao, M. Georgeff, BDI Agents: from theory to practice. In V. Lesser, editor, Proceedings of the First International Conference on Multi-Agent Systems (IC-MAS'95), pages 312-319. The MIT Press: Cambridge, MA, USA, 1995.

11. K. Sycara, J. Giampapa, B. Langley, M. Paolucci. "The RETSINA MAS, a Case Study." 2003. SELMAS, vol. LNCS 2603, edited by A. Garcia, C. Lucena, F. Zambonelli, A. Omici, and J. Castro, 232-50. NewYork: Springer-Verlag.

12. K. Sycara, K. Decker, A. Pannu, M. Williamson, "Distributed Intelligent Agents," IEEE Expert, 11(6):36–46, December 1996.

Resource Optimization in Multi-Display Environments with Distributed GRASP

Thomas Heider, Martin Giersich, and Thomas Kirste

Mobile Multimedia Information Systems Group
Rostock University, Germany
{th,mg,tk}@informatik.uni-rostock.de

Abstract. Emerging multiple display infrastructures provide users with a large number of semi-public and private displays. Selecting what information to present on which display here becomes a real issue, especially when multiple users with diverging interests have to be considered. This especially holds for *dynamic* ensembles of displays.

We propose to cast the *Display Mapping problem* as an optimization task. We develop an explicit criterion for the global quality of a display mapping and then describe a distributed algorithm based on the GRASP framework that is able to approximate the global optimum through local interaction between display devices. We claim that such a distributed optimization approach, based on the definition of an explicit global quality measure, is a general concept for achieving coherent ensemble behavior.

1 Introduction

"(...) for each person in an office, there should be hundreds of tabs, tens of pads, and one or two boards" Mark Weiser, 1993 [1]

Since Weiser's vision, displays have begun to proliferate. For people coming together in a well equipped meeting room, the above numbers of devices are not quite achieved yet – but we seem to be getting close. Multiple display environments are an active research topic[1] and we are moving towards environments that provide a substantial number of public and personal displays to a user. Figure 1 shows some typical scenarios (Stanford's iRoom [7] and our own lab[2]) for illustration.

Multiple display environments create an interesting challenge: The *Display Mapping problem* – that is, deciding which information to present on what display in order to optimally satisfy the users' needs for information. While this task is more or less trivial in single-user, single-display situations, it becomes challenging in multi-user, multi-display settings: Users and displays are spatially dispersed so that the visibility of (semi-) public and private displays varies across

---

[1] See for instance the UbiComp 2004 workshop on Ubiquitous Display Environments [2], specifically [3–6].

[2] Note to reviewers: This lab is currently under construction and being finished in May 2006. A final version of this paper will refer to this lab.

Fig. 1. Multi-display environments: Stanford's iRoom (left), our own lab (right, under construction)

users. Also, information needs may vary across users, so that finding the "best" assignment of information to displays becomes a typical optimization problem. To our knowledge, the development of an interaction-free, automatic display assignment has not yet been addressed on a general level (i.e., independent of a specific ensemble).

How does one solve an optimization problem? – By defining the objective function $q(x)$, the "quality", to maximize and then applying a suitable optimization algorithm to compute $x_{max} = \arg \max_{x \in X} q(x)$.

So the Display Mapping problem gives rise to two subproblems:

– What is a suitable definition for $q(x)$? I.e., what is the objective function to be maximized in order to achieve an optimal (or at least: satisfactory) solution for the Display Mapping problem?
– How should the computation of x_{max} be distributed across the members of an ensemble of displays? – This is especially interesting, when dynamic ensembles have to be considered (e.g., portable projectors carried into a meeting room, etc.).

Before we embark on the details: Why should these questions be interesting? – Couldn't the users just do the assignment manually, using a suitable interactive interface? (e.g., dragging document icons onto display icons, as outlined in [8]? Or using the PointRight software developed for Stanford's Meyer Teamspace [9]?) We do not believe that such a solution would be successful in the long run (i.e., as multiple display environments become more and more complex):

1. Interest conflicts between users will always need a computer supported negotiation mechanism.
2. The need for dynamic realignment of Display Mapping is caused by topic changes in the user population – in this situation, the user's focus of attention will be on the changing topic rather than on convincing the display infrastructure to change the topic[3].

---

[3] The classical counter-example: The next speaker mounts the stage, and instead of delivering a speech, he starts fidgeting with his notebook in order to get his presentation onto the screen ...

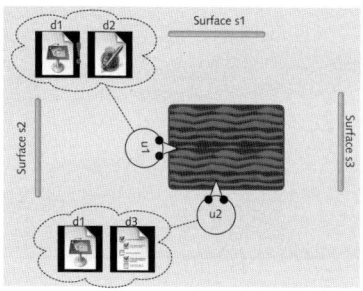 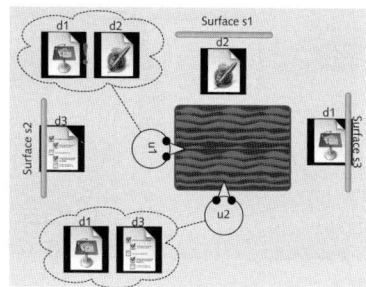

Fig. 2. Mapping documents to displays. Initial situation (left) and optimal mapping (right)

3. In a dynamic multiple display environment, the user will not *be able* to know (and will not want to know) the displays currently available to him. With dozens to hundreds of possible display configurations, the user will want to rely on the infrastructure to select the best choice for him.

We call a solution process that does not require human intervention an *unsupervised* process. In this paper, we discuss some ideas for the unsupervised solution of the Display Mapping problem for dynamic multiple display environments.

With respect to this topic, the contributions of our paper are:

1. The proposal of a function q that provides a precise definition of a *globally optimal* display mapping in a multiple display environment.
2. The proposal of a distributed optimization algorithm that requires only *local knowledge* at each participating device. (This algorithm is applicable to arbitrary objective functions q.)
3. And, at the meta level, the observation that some aspects of a globally coherent behavior of a dynamic ensemble of ubicomp devices can be treated as optimization problems.

The further structure of this paper is as follows: in Section 2, we outline the display mapping problem and our definition of a global quality function q for this problem. In Section 3, we discuss a possible strategy for approximating q in a dynamic ensemble of devices and outline our algorithmic solution. Experimental results regarding the achievable quality and the required computational effort are reported in Section 4. A discussion of the results and further work is given in Section 5.

2   Defining Optimal Display Assignment

2.1   The Basic Idea

Consider the simple Display Mapping problem outlined in Figure 2, left. There are two users u_1, u_2 sitting at a table and three display surfaces s_1, s_2, s_3 (for

instance, backprojection displays or simply screens with an associated projector).
User u_1 is interested in documents d_1 and d_2, user u_2 is interested in d_1 and d_3.
Also, u_1 has very high interest in d_1 (maybe it is the presentation currently
delivered by u_2). In this situation, considering the positions of users and display
surfaces, the resulting display visibility, and the user's information needs, an
optimal mapping of documents to the available display surfaces is given by the
mapping outlined in Figure 2 at right: u_1 gets optimal visibility of his most
important document on s_3 and acceptable visibility of d_2 by looking sideways
on s_1. Similarly u_2, gets acceptable visibility of d_1 and d_3.

Let D, U, S be the sets of documents, users, and surfaces, respectively. Let
$impt(d, u) \in [0..1]$ denote the importance of the document $d \in D$ to a user
$u \in U$ and $vis(s, u) \in [0..1]$ the visibility of surface $s \in S$ by user $u \in U$. Let
furthermore $sm \in D \rightarrow 2^S$ be a mapping of documents to display surfaces,
such that $sm(d) \in 2^S$ denotes the set of surfaces to which document $d \in D$ is
assigned[4]. Then the quality achieved by the mapping sm can simply be defined
as

$$q(sm) = \sum_{\substack{u \in U \\ d \in D}} impt(d, u) * \max_{s \in sm(d)} vis(s, u) \qquad (1)$$

This definition is based on the unsurprising intuition that, in a good mapping,

$$q(dm, ym) = \sum_{\substack{u \in U \\ d \in D}} impt(d, u) * \max_{y \in dm(d)} \left(vis(ym(y), u) * rend(y, ym(y)) \right) \qquad (2)$$

Fig. 3. Maximum Quality Function

documents with high importance (for specific users) should be assigned to display
surfaces with high visibility (for this user). In addition, if a document is assigned
to multiple display surfaces, only the best one for a given user is considered when
computing the quality for this user (this is the "max vis" term).

Finding the optimal mapping $sm_{max} = \arg\max_{sm \in D \rightarrow 2^S} q(sm)$ requires to explore
the possible document-to-surface maps in a suitable manner in order to find
surface map giving the best quality.

2.2   Accounting for Different Types of Displays

Since some time, steerable projectors such as the Everywhere Display [10] are
being investigated for a flexible information display by several research groups
(see [4] for a short overview). And our lab infrastructure too provides such a device (cf. Figure 4). The introduction of steerable projectors introduces another
degree of freedom in the display mapping process, as a steerable projector may

---

[4] Clearly, it sometimes makes sense to display a document on more than one display
surface.

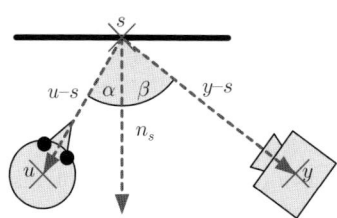 

Fig. 4. Visibility & Projectability; our Steerable Projector

be able to choose between different projection screens. We therefore need to distinguish between *Displays* (devices which can present a document) and *Surfaces* (regions in space on which a display renders a document). For some devices, the mapping from display to surface is fixed (i.e., a notebook display will always render on the notebook's screen surface; a fixed beamer will always render on the screen it is looking at), while for other devices it is variable (i.e., a steerable beamer that can pick different screens to project on).

Let Y denote the set of displays and S the set of available (display) surfaces. Furthermore, let $rend(y, s) \in [0..1]$ be the rendering quality achievable by display $y \in Y$ on surface $s \in S$ (for devices with fixed display surface, *rend* will be 1 for this surface and 0 everywhere else). We now have to replace *sm* by *two* mappings: $dm \in D \to 2^Y$, mapping documents to sets of display devices, and $ym \in Y \to S$, mapping displays to surfaces. And our definition of q is changed to – see **Figure 3** – so that we now have to look for $(dm_{max}, ym_{max}) = \arg\max_{\substack{dm \in D \to 2^Y \\ ym \in Y \to S}} q(dm, ym)$. As a first approximation to computing *vis* and *rend*, we have chosen Lambert's law of reflection, which gives the visibility (or rendering quality) as cosine of the angle between the rendering surfaces' surface normal n_s and the vector connecting the surface and the projector (resp. the user) – see Figure 4, left. A similar approach has been taken by the EasyLiving Geometry model [11].

We would like to emphasize two points with respect to our definition of q:

– q has been defined completely independent from a concrete ensemble of users, displays, documents, and surfaces. It describes the globally optimal behavior for any possible ensemble. Once machinery is available for computing the optimum for q, any ensemble will be able to behave optimally – as far as q is a correct definition of an ensembles global optimum from the user's point of view.

– Clearly, our definition of q for the display mapping problem is a rather simplistic one – for instance, it lacks a notion of "history", that would keep a document from confusingly hopping from display to display as the user slightly shifts position. So, q does not yet faithfully describe an ensemble's global optimum from the user's point of view. Our objective has not been to already provide a final q (which would also require substantial user studies), but first to show that an ensemble globally optimal behavior *can* (and should!) be defined explicitly in a way that is independent of a specific ensemble realization.

In the next section, we will look at mechanisms that allow an ensemble to approximate a global optimum defined by a function such as q in a way that requires only local knowledge from each ensemble member.

3   Distributed Optimization in ad-hoc Ensembles

Due to the fast growing search space – if we add more components like displays and surfaces or documents – and the time limit to find an optimal mapping, it is not possible to iterate over the whole search space. The mapping problem of our smart meeting room example is a problem where the solution is encoded with discrete variables and belongs therefore to the class of combinatorial optimization problems. For this kind of problems, many different metaheuristics are proposed [12]. Fundamental properties to select an appropriate metaheuristic are completeness and efficiency. The goal is to find a method that efficiently explores the search space in order to find (near-) optimal solutions in the shortest possible time.

But in the scenario of document display mapping there are special requirements to the search process. We have different autonomous components: projectors, surfaces, documents, users: we have a naturally distributed problem. Distributed optimization problems are problems where each variable and constraint is owned by an agent. Traditionally, such problems were gathered into a single place and a centralized algorithm was applied in order to find a solution. However, distributed optimization has a number of practical advantages over its centralized counterpart.

Centralized optimization is in our case infeasible due to privacy and data integration problems. As few as possible information should be exchanged between components and / or stored stored centrally. There may be components that do not wish to reveal specific information about themselves. Furthermore, it may be difficult for a (central) component to compute internal properties of other components. Take for example the calculation of the visibility by *vis*. Only the surface component may have the needed algorithm to calculate its visibility faithfully. If, for instance, two screens have a different gain-factor, then the visibility is different, even if the viewing angle and distance from the user to the screens is the same. In a fully distributed, local-knowledge approach, each surface is free to use its own tailored version of *vis*. In a centralized approach, these individual computations need to be shipped to (and evaluated by) the central component. The same drawback applies to classical distributed optimization approaches that just distribute the iterations of the optimization procedure or different slices of the search space (*e.g.*, [13]) across the available computing nodes: here too all nodes need global knowledge to assess the contribution of all available components to solutions in their iteration or search space slice.

The dynamic of the system is another reason. New components added ad-hoc, like notebooks oder mobile projectors, must be included in the search space. That means, by the time we would have centralized the problem, it has already changed. Furthermore, the computing power of the different components is limited. We could not guarantee that there is a component in a dynamic created ensemble which would have the resources to compute the optimization problem alone.

3.1   The Search Space

If we look at the goal function (Eq. 2), we see that it is searching for the maximum of two assignments. The first mapping is the assignment of documents to displays, e.g., projectors (dm), whereas the other mapping is the assignment of projectors to surfaces (ym). The search space consist of all possible assignments of both maps (DM, YM). The number of the possible assignments is given by the number of projectors, surfaces and documents. The cardinalities of the maps are as follows:

- Document-Display-Map: $\#D^{\#Y}$

- Display-Surface-Map: $\binom{v}{w}$,
  where $v = \max(\#Y, \#S), w = \min(\#Y, \#S)$

As we can see, if we have a larger number of components, the search space will grow rapidly.

Before we describe the optimization algorithms we used, we will discuss some considerations which have influenced our algorithms approach.

The first point is that, although we are looking for two separate maps (Display $\rightarrow$ Surface; Document $\rightarrow$ Display), we can not calculate these maps independently. Consider for instance the left sketch of Figure 5. Assume there would only be the projector p_2. If the Display-Surface map is computed independently, then p_2 would always inevitably choose surface s_1, because this gives the best value for *rend*. With this choice, it is then impossible to arrive at the true maximum for q, as the user is looking at surface s_2.

Another problem are local maxima. A trivial example is displayed in the left and middle picture of Figure 5. Although the projector p_2 has a maximum projectability onto surface s_1, the overall maximum projectability is achieved when projector p_2 is directed to surface s_2. A somewhat more complex scenario is given in the right[5] picture of Fig. 5. Assume that the importance of document d_0 is for all users somewhat higher than the importance of document d_1, e.g. $\forall u \in U : imp(d_0, u) = 0.8 \wedge imp(d_1, u) = 0.6$. In this constellation it is then better to display the more important document d_0 on the surfaces s_1 and s_2, and the less important document d_1 on surface s_3, because the users are looking directly at s_1 and s_2 respectively. If an algorithm would choose to display d_0 on surface s_3, which would be the initial choice in a greedy approach, it could not reach the

---

[5] The right drawing of Figure 5 shows test room 6. See tables of the result section.

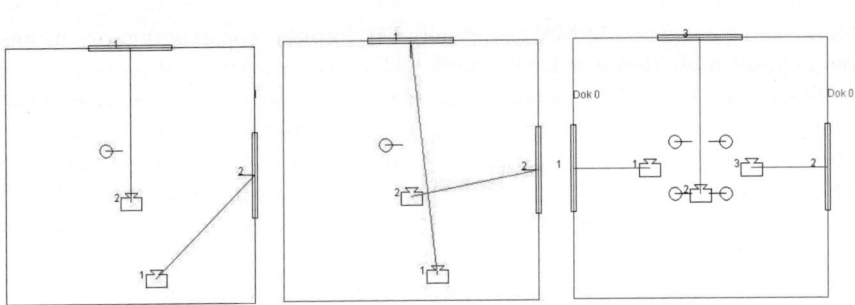

Fig. 5. Simple examples for discussion of the search space

global optimum anymore. Greedy best-first algorithms tend to become stuck in the region around a local optimum.

We used these example to choose an appropriate algorithm and also for testing the performance. We decided to use GRASP as starting point for our first distribution algorithm, because it meets our search space requirements and it seemed reasonably straightforward to transform GRASP into a fully distributed local-knowledge optimization procedure. For comparison, we used an auction based approach.

3.2 GRASP

Greedy Randomized Adaptive Search Procedures are metaheuristic methods for combinatorial problems (*e.g.*[14]). GRASP combines the advantages of a greedy proceeding for a search of good solutions with the positive features of randomizing to cover a wide area of the search space. GRASP is mostly implemented as a multi-start or iterative process, in which each iteration consists basically of two phases: a construction phase and a local search phase (*e.g.*, hill climbing). The construction phase incrementally builds a feasible initial solution, whose neighborhood is investigated until a local optimum is found during the the local search phase.

At each iteration of the construction phase, the set of candidate elements will be formed by all elements that can be incorporated to the partial solution under construction without destroying feasibility. The selection of the next element for incorporation is determined by the evaluation of all candidate elements according to a greedy evaluation function. The evaluation of the elements by this function leads to the creation of a restricted candidate list (RCL), formed by the k best elements[6]. The element to be incorporated into the partial solution is randomly selected from those in the RCL. This random selection ensures

---

[6] For conciseness, we outline only the cardinality-based RCL construction. See [15] for a more thorough treatment.

sufficient variability in the construction phase, providing wide area coverage of the search space.

The solutions generated by the greedy randomized construction are in most cases not optimal. Hence a local search phase follows, which usually improves the constructed solution. A local search algorithm works in an iterative fashion by successively replacing the current solution by a better solution in the neighborhood of the current solution. It terminates when no better solution is found in the neighborhood. One iteration of the GRASP algorithm is now finished. In the case of the multi-start variant, the whole procedure will be iterated until a given criteria is reached, which can be the maximum number of iterations, a timeout or a minimum quality. The best overall solution is kept as the result.

3.3   Distributing GRASP

As mentioned earlier, we need a fully distributed local knowledge version of the optimization algorithm. Our approach, the distributed GRASP algorithm (DGRASP), operates in three main phases outlined below.

Initialization Phase. We consider every component of our scenario (displays, surfaces, documents, users) as an individual agent. Every component of the room that joints the appliance ensemble broadcasts the information needed by the other components (*e.g.*, type, position, normal vector, rotation ability (steerable projector), document importance etc.). In our current implementation, the surface agents are the main components for the DGRASP implementation. Surfaces will collect the relevant information about users, documents, and displays and they will note the presence of other surfaces. Surfaces themselves do not exchange any information about their capabilities, so that surfaces act purely locally with respect to other surfaces[7].

Construction Phase. DGRASP itself starts with the distributed generation of a feasible initial solution. The construction algorithm (Alg. 1) consists of the following steps:

1 – **MakeLocalRCL.** Starting from the current partial solution s^* (which is empty at the begining), every surface agent a generates several extended partial solutions by choosing a display $y \in Y$ and a document $d \in D$ and adding the the mapping $y \mapsto a$ and $d \mapsto \{y\}$ to the current display-surface resp. the current document-display maps of s^*.

   Using the definition of q, the quality of these extended partial solutions will be calculated. Accordingly to the quality value, the k best solutions are put into the Restricted Candidate List.

2 – **SelectRandom.** Every agent choses randomly one solution from its local RCL.

---

[7] The fact that surfaces need to know about the capabilities of displays is a clear violation of the locality principle we try to achieve – and an obvious shortcoming of our current implementation.

```
Executed by Every Agent i:
s* := {};
while Broadcast ≠ NIL received do
    s_i := s*;
    RCL := MakeLocalRCL(s_i);
    if RCL ≠ {} then
        s_i' := s_i + SelectRandom(RCL);
        Broadcast(s_i')
    else
        Broadcast(NIL)
    end
    Receive(s_j) from other Agents a_j;
    s* := max(s_j);
end
```

Algorithm 1: DGRASP Construction Phase

```
Executed by Every Agent:
v := value(s*);
repeat
    v* := v;
    s_i := s*;
    s_i' := LocalSelectBest(Steps(s_i));
    Broadcast(<s_i', value(s_i')>);
    Receive(<s_j, value(s_j)>) from other Agents a_j;
    v := max(value(s_j));
    s* := s_j where value(s_j) = v
until v* = v ;
```

Algorithm 2: DGRASP Local Search Phase

3 – Broadcast. This extended partial solution is broadcast to all other surface agents in the ensemble.

4 – SelectMax. All agents now have a synchronized list of all extended partial solutions. Each agent selects the best from this list as new current solution s^*.

Steps 1–4 are repeated until all surfaces resp. displays are assigned. Then the construction phase ends and the local search phase begins.

Local Search Phase. Local search (Alg. 2) operates on a complete solution and tries to improve it using the following steps:

1 – LocalSelectBest. Every surface agent exchanges the document assigned to its surface and calculates the new resulting quality value of that solution. It does this with all documents and consequently it selects the best new solution. If there is no quality gain, the old solution is retained.

2 – Broadcast. Broadcast of the created solution to all other surface agents in the ensemble.

3 – SelectMax. All agents have now a synchronized list of all proposals for improved solutions. They then locally select the best proposal based on the quality value.

Steps 1 – 3 are repeated until no better solution is broadcasted by any agent. This process implements *hill climbing* as local search, i.e., the algorithm moves deterministically in the local neighborhood of the current solution towards the local maximum.

One iteration of the GRASP algorithm is now finished. Since GRASP is a multi-start approach, the whole procedure will be repeated n times (*e.g.*, $n = 5$). After finishing the last iteration, the solution with the best quality value of all iterations is the final result.

3.4 Running DGRASP

A rough sketch of the messages communicated between the components during a run of DGRASP is given in Table 1. This "trace" is based on a subset of the problem shown in Figure 2. The message structure is defined below. First the messages for exchange of context information are shown.

$$User_{context} = (uid, [imap = (uid, \{did \mapsto ivalue\})], [amap = (uid, \{did \mapsto avalue\})])$$
$$Document_{context} = \{(did, name)\}$$
$$displaY_{context} = (yid, pos = (x, y, z), normal = (x, y, z), res = (x, y))$$
$$Surface_{context} = (sid, pos = (x, y, z), normal = (x, y, z), size = (width, height))$$

uid, did, yid, and sid are unique numbers identifying the individual components. $imap$ is the importance-map, a list of key-value-pairs where the keys are document-identiers, and the values range between 0 and 1. The access-map $amap$ connects the same key-values to access-rights. The other variables $pos, normal, res$, and $size$ are straightforward.

In the next section, we will look at the performance achievable with DGRASP with respect to the solution quality achieved and the number of messages required.

4   Experimental Results

4.1   DGRASP Evaluation

To benchmark DGRASP, we created 10 different test rooms on which DGRASP has been run using a simulation system. The rooms differ in respect to number and positions of the relevant components. We have tried to create a large diversity in the room design, so that the spectrum varies from awkward constellations to optimal constellations. Examples of these rooms are shown in Figure 6 and in the right sketch of Figure 5.

In our tests, the algorithms were executed 100 times per room. In every run, the constellation of the respective room, including the positions of the users, were constant, but new documents with new importance values were created. These experimental setting should guarantee a realistic validation of the algorithms.

Table 1. Messages sent by the individual appliance components to acchieve the goal of an optimized document-display-mapping with distributed GRASP

Initialization: Components broadcast context information on context channel		
Users	U_1	$(u1, imap = (u1, \{d1 \mapsto 0.8, d2 \mapsto 0.6\}),$
		$amap = (u1, \{d1 \mapsto 777, d2 \mapsto 777\}))$
	U_2	$(u2, imap = (u2, \{d1 \mapsto 0.6, d2 \mapsto 0.8\}),$
		$amap = (u2, \{d1 \mapsto 777, d2 \mapsto 777\}))$
Projectors	Y_1	$(y1, pos = (0.0, 0.5, 0.6), normal = (1.0, 0.0, 0.0), res = (1280, 854))$
	Y_2	$(y2, pos = (0.75, 0.0, 0.6), normal = (0.0, 1.0, 0.0), res = (1280, 854))$
Screens	S_1	$(s1, pos = (1, 0.5, 0.6), normal = (-1.0, 0.0, 0.0), size = (80, 60))$
	S_3	$(s3, pos = (0.75, 1.0, 0.6), normal = (0.0, -1.0, 0.0), size = (80, 60))$
Construction phase: incremental creation of a initial solution		
construct...	S_1	$(s1, solution = (\{y1 \mapsto s1\}, \{d1 \mapsto \{y1\}\}, 1.0, C))$
	S_3	$(s3, solution = (\{y1 \mapsto s3\}, \{d2 \mapsto \{y1\}\}, 0.8, C))$
after receiving the initial solutions, $S_{1,3}$ improve solutions		
construct...	S_1	$(s1, solution = (\{y1 \mapsto s1\}, \{d1 \mapsto \{y1\}\}, 1.0, C))$
	S_3	$(s3, solution = (\{y1 \mapsto s1, y2 \mapsto s3\}, \{d1 \mapsto \{y1\}, d1 \mapsto \{y2\}\}, 1.8, C))$
Local search: improving current solution by searching the neighborhood		
local search...	S_1	$(s1, solution = (\{y1 \mapsto s1, y2 \mapsto s3\}, \{d2 \mapsto \{y1\}, d1 \mapsto \{y2\}\}, 2.1, L))$
	S_3	$(s3, solution = (\{y1 \mapsto s1, y2 \mapsto s3\}, \{d1 \mapsto \{y1\}, d2 \mapsto \{y2\}\}, 1.8, L))$
choose best solution for improvement of local search		
local search...	S_1	$(s1, solution = (\{y1 \mapsto s1, y2 \mapsto s3\}, \{d2 \mapsto \{y1\}, d1 \mapsto \{y2\}\}, 2.1, L))$
	S_3	$(s3, solution = (\{y1 \mapsto s1, y2 \mapsto s3\}, \{d2 \mapsto \{y1\}, d1 \mapsto \{y2\}\}, 2.1, L))$
local search is finished, no further refinement possible		
Multi-start: begin with new construction phase until max. iterations reached		
DGRASP solution: $(\{y1 \mapsto s1, y2 \mapsto s3\}, \{d2 \mapsto \{y1\}, d1 \mapsto \{y2\}\})$		

Table 2 gives the mean μ and the standard deviation σ of the solution quality achieved in the test runs. The solution quality is given relative to the true optimum ($= 100$), computed by an exhaustive search of the solution space. The mean is a direct indicator for the average quality of the algorithms, while the standard deviation is a measurement for the robustness of the algorithm: the smaller the standard deviation, the more stable is the quality of the result.

We have tested DGRASP with two different parameter settings. DGRASP1_1 is run with $n = 1$ and $k = 1$, i.e., a single iteration with a restricted candidate list of length 1. DGRASP5_2 has been run with $n = 5$ restarts a candidate list length of $k = 2$.

To get a feeling for the general performance of our DGRASP algorithm, we have compared DGRASP to a simple auction based [16] display assignment

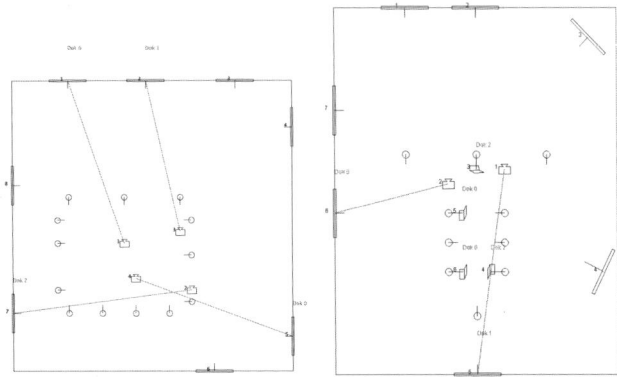

Fig. 6. Test rooms number 4 and 5

algorithm. The basic concept of this method in our display mapping scenario is the creation of the maps with auctions between the participating components.

Our naive auction mechanism is rather inferior to DGRASP with respect to quality, but this method seems to be quite effective considering the communication overhead: Table 3 displays the number of messages that were needed to execute the algorithms. This is a good indicator for the performance of the procedures in real world wireless infrastructures.

Table 2. Average relative quality (mean, μ) and standard deviation (σ) of the solutions in relation to the global optimum in %

# test room	DGRASP1_1		DGRASP5_2		AUCTION	
	μ	σ	μ	σ	μ	σ
1	98.32	1.19	97.78	1.25	94.16	2.53
2	98.47	1.27	98.22	1.41	84.53	7.56
3	98.49	1.51	98.57	1.57	91.12	5.48
4	98.70	1.47	98.01	1.49	92.69	5.55
5	97.14	2.16	98.54	1.61	71.38	18.32
6	96.61	2.82	99.36	1.88	86.79	9.83
7	89.93	8.05	99.06	1.90	77.20	13.18
8	98.06	4.15	97.53	2.09	91.95	11.61
9	98.19	4.06	99.59	2.16	82.60	10.46
10	99.19	4.22	99.55	2.07	85.73	9.51

The experiments show that the DGRASP1_1 parametrization already provides passably good results. But the missing randomization (RCL length $k = 1$) results in a high standard deviation and sometimes poor qualties (see *e.g.*, test room 7). DGRASP1_1 apparently sometimes gets stuck in regions around local maxima. The DGRASP5_2 parametrization, true multi-start in conjunction

Table 3. Average number of communications during the whole search procedure

# test room	DGRASP1_1	DGRASP5_2	AUCTION
1	642	3315	225
2	645	3343	225
3	1216	6341	391
4	1233	6215	422
5	1540	7973	568
6	105	552	75
7	728	3721	195
8	394	2040	172
9	886	4720	329
10	2364	11882	306

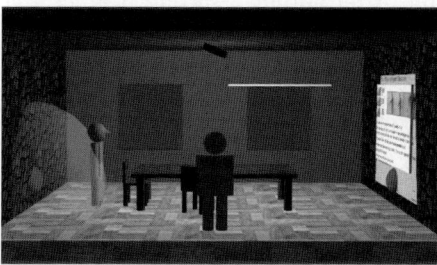 

Fig. 7. Environment Simulation System

with the randomization of the RCL during the construction phase, delivers the required variability to browse the search space. The constant good quality and the small standard deviation allows the conclusion that DGRASP with 5 restarts and a RCL with 2 candidates will be appropriate for multi-display constellations we can find in meeting rooms.

The disadvantages of the present implementation of the DGRASP algorithm is the low distribution of the procedure. Only the surfaces are actively involved in the search procedure and split the calculations among each other. The other components serve only as information providers. We are currently working on a modified version that will also make the display agents active components (thereby avoiding the violation of the locality principle that surfaces currently need to understand the capabilities of displays).

The experiments with the auction based method produced no satisfactory results with respect to quality. We need to look deeper into useful auction mechanisms in order to give this approach a fair chance against DGRASP. What is interesting with the auction procedure is the significantly lower amount of messages that was needed in comparison to DGRASP. This justifies a further investigation of the market based approach.

4.2   Environment Simulator

For a first informal evaluation of the applicability of our approach from the user's point of view, we have built a simple environment simulator. This is a visual simulation tool for smart / instrumented environments that provides a simple rendering & physics simulation server, to which all components of our system (mostly java agents) can connect via sockets. The environment simulator is able to visualize the devices in the room and to display their behavior (*e.g.*, to project a document onto a wall). Furthermore, the simulator can be programmed to provide a test room with an environment geometry, sensor data, simulated users with a dedicated behavior, and interior. So it is possible to use this simulator to visually inspect the behavior of a typical ensemble controlled by q.

In the two pictures of Fig. 7, we have illustrated such an example. In the left image we have a scene with one steerable projector, one screen, and two users, where user to the right gives a presentation. After adding a second beamer and two notebooks, the ensemble calculates a remapping of the document display assignment (based on the maximum quality function of Eq. 2), resulting in th display mapping shown in Figure 7 at right. Initial results using the environment simulator system hint that q and its DGRASP approximation provide plausible behavior – this is no replacement for a user study, but an encouragement that pursuing our approach is worthwhile.

5   Conclusion

To summarize, we make the following claims:

- The coherence of the behavior of an ensemble of devices can – for certain cooperation problems such as the Display Mapping – be represented by a global quality measure that is independent from the specific makeup of an ensemble. Any ensemble that maximizes this quality measure will exhibit coherence with respect to the user needs represented by this quality measure.
- The maximization of the coherence realized by an ensemble can be achieved by a completely distributed optimization process that requires only local knowledge from every device in the ensemble. A device only needs to be able to assess its own contribution to the solution provided by the ensemble.

  Complete distribution and locality are inevitable requirements created by the dynamic nature of ad-hoc ensembles.

We think that this approach is applicable to other aspects of coherent ensemble behavior as well – for instance, optimizing illumination.

Some additional aspects are worth mentioning:

- In order for this approach to be applicable in the real world, q has to represent the user expectations faithfully. Developing a suitable quality measure will require significant user studies. With respect to display mapping, these studies are planned for the future.

  For these user studies we are currently building a dedicated experimental infrastructure (Note to reviewer: we expect first results by September).

- Currently, our simple DGRASP algorithm seems to be a better approach (providing a higher global quality on average) than an auction-based mechanism. However, the auction-based mechanism uses much less communication, hinting at a significantly better scaling capability. We need further investigation with respect to designing a better auction mechanism as well as with respect to reducing the communication overhead of DGRASP.
  Also, we need to understand how to better control the main factors in an ensemble's composition that drive the complexity of the optimization problem.
- Is this all worth the effort? I.e., will the user notice, if we just achieve 80% quality rather than 95%? – Although a well-founded answer is possible only after user studies, we think: yes. Why? Because already small deviations from the global optimum result in a different display mapping, immediately noticeable to the user and violating his expectation. Users might be tempted to correct the system manually, which can require more effort (changing all mappings manually) than saved by the system – the well known "obtrusive paper clip assistance" syndrome.

References

1. Weiser, M.: Some computer science issues in ubiquitous computing. Communications of the ACM **36**(7) (1993) 75–84
2. Ferscha, A., Kortuem, G., Krüger, A.: Workshop on ubiquitous display environments. In: Proc. Ubicomp 2004, Nottingham, England (2004)
3. Hutchings, D.R., Czerwinski, M., Meyers, B., Stasko, J.: Exploring the use and affordances of multiple display environments. [2]
4. Molyneaux, D., Kortuem, G.: Ubiquitous displays in dynamic environments: Issues and opportunities. [2]
5. Schmidt, R., Penner, E., Carpendale, S.: Reconfigurable displays. [2]
6. Summet, J.W., et al.: Robust projected displays for ubiquitous computing. [2]
7. Johanson, B., Fox, A., Winograd, T.: The interactive workspaces project: Experiences with ubiquitous computing rooms. IEEE Pervasive Computing (2002)
8. Nazari Shirehjini, A.: A Generic UPnP Architecture for Ambient Intelligence Meeting Rooms and a Control Pont allowing for integrated 2D and 3D interaction. In: Proc. Smart Objects & Ambient Intelligence (sOc-EUSAI 2005), Grenoble, France (2005)
9. Johanson, B., Hutchins, G., Winograd, T., Stone, M.: Pointright: Experience with flexible input redirection in interactive workspaces. In: Proc. ACM Conference on User Interface and Software Technology (UIST2002), Paris, France (2002) 227–234
10. Pinhanez, C.: The everywhere displays projector: A device to create ubiquitous graphical interfaces. In: Proc. of Ubiquitous Computing 2001 (Ubicomp'01), Atlanta, USA (2001)
11. Brumitt, B., Shafer, S.: Better living through geometry. Journal for Ubiquitous Computing (2001)
12. Blum, C., Roli, A.: Metaheuristics in combinatorial optimization: Overview and conceptual comparison. ACM Computing Surveys **35**(3) (2003) 268–308
13. Modi, P., Shen, W., Tambe, M., Yokoo, M.: Adopt: Asynchronous distributed constraint optimization with quality guarantees. In: Artificial Intelligence Journal(AIJ). Volume 161. (2005) 149–180

14. Feo, T.A., Resende, M.G.C.: Greedy randomized adaptive search procedures. Journal of Global Optimization **6** (1995) 109–133
15. Pitsoulis, L.S., Resende, M.G.C.: Greedy randomized adaptive search procedures. In Pardalos, P.M., Resende, M.G.C., eds.: Handbook of Applied Optimization. Oxford University Press (2002) 168–183
16. Schwartz, R., Kraus, S.: Bidding mechanisms for data allocation in multi-agent environments. In: Agent Theories, Architectures, and Languages. (1997) 61–75

Strengthening the Security of Machine Readable Documents by Combining RFID and Optical Memory Devices

Mikko Lehtonen[1], Florian Michahelles[1], Thorsten Staake[2], and Elgar Fleisch[1,2]

[1] Information Management, ETH Zurich, 8092 Zurich, Switzerland
{initial+lastname}@ethz.ch
[2] Institute of Technology Management, University of St.Gallen, 9000 St.Gallen, Switzerland
{firstname.lastname}@unisg.ch

Abstract. There is an on-going trend towards turning paper documents that store personal information or other valuable data into machine-readable form. An example of this trend is the electronic passport that will become common in the near future. In this paper we show how the security of these machine readable documents could be improved by combining RFID with optical memory devices. We propose integrating an optical memory device into the RFID enabled smart document and present methods how these two storage media can be combined to secure the document against threats like illicit scanning, eavesdropping and forgery. The presented approaches make use of the optical document-to-reader channel which is more secure than the radio-frequency communication interface. To demonstrate the potential of our approaches we show how they could overcome a number of existing security and privacy threats of electronic passports.

1   Introduction

Radio frequency identification (RFID) is an important enabling technique of ambient intelligence. In applications like supply chain management it is used as a mere labeling technique [25], while in anti-counterfeiting its role is for example to implement cryptographic challenge-response authentication protocol [23]. As RFID technology becomes more and more pervasive and closer to our everyday life, also the discussion of the relating security and privacy risks increases. Indeed, addressing the security and privacy threats is of great importance for the acceptance and adoption of RFID [30, 28]

Integration of RFID transponders into physical documents has lead to evolution of machine readable documents. The best known application of this field is the electronic passport, or *e-passport*, where an RFID transponder is used to store biometric data of the passport's holder. Millions of e-passports are already in the circulation today [16] and the number will keep increasing – the U.S. alone will issue more than seven million e-passports each year starting from October 2006 [11, 12].

There are numerous applications where tagging physical documents would be interesting: besides e-passports and other travel documents, also for example customs freight papers, security papers (e.g. gift certificates, jewelry appraisals), driver's licenses and vehicle registration papers would benefit from being machine readable through radio-frequency (RF) communication. A common factor of these documents is that they all relate to a physical entity that is not very well suited to be tagged to become a data carrier itself: integrating RFID chips into an expensive jewelry, for example, might conflict with its classical, non-technical nature. Also, besides some extreme cases , tagging of human beings is not likely to happen. Therefore, even though objects are turning into data carriers through integration of ambient intelligence technologies, there is and will be a need also for separate data carrier documents.

In this paper we propose new ways of combining RFID with optical memory devices to increase the security of machine readable documents. Our goal is to evaluate and show different approaches of the combined use of these devices. It should be noted that throughout this paper we refer to RFID devices in a broad sense that comprises also contactless smart cards. We propose and evaluate four different approaches how this combination could be used to overcome existing security threats of machine readable documents in terms of more secure communication protocols and resistance against forgery and cloning. Instead of establishing security based on sharing secrets between the reader device and document before the communication, we make use of optical memory devices which cannot be read or eavesdropped without a line of sight.

This paper is organized as follows. In section 2 we discuss machine readable documents in general. A general model of the technical infrastructure for RFID enabled machine readable documents is presented in subsection 2.1 and an overview to travel documents in subsection 2.2. The security and privacy of machine readable travel documents is discussed in subsection 2.3. Section 3 presents optical memory devices and four approaches how we combine them with RFID in physical documents to achieve specific security objectives. In section 4 we discuss the security of the proposed communication models and we finish with conclusions.

2   Machine Readable Documents

Physical documents can be made machine readable by integrating RFID transponders into them. This creates a link between the physical world and the virtual world and can extend the role of the documents. Within this paper we denote all physical documents that carry a digital memory device as machine readable documents. The typical instance of these kinds of documents is an RFID tagged paper. Another way to make documents machine readable is to use optical character recognition (OCR) to read data printed on the document.

In existing and proposed applications RFID tags are integrated into documents to enable automated document tracking [13], to increase the security of the documents [24, 17] and in general to improve the document handling processes, like the biometric authentication using e-passports [8]. The possible applications of machine readable documents are as manifold as those of normal documents, and more. This is made possible by the digital storage and, optionally, by the logic of the integrated circuits.

The benefits of having RFID transponders in physical documents come from the simple and fast read processes that does not demand a line of sight connection. Depending on the grade and price of the chip, the contactless memory device can also support for re-writable memory and logical functions like cryptographic primitives. Therefore machine readable documents can also provide high level of security and counterfeit resistance.

The following subsection presents the general technical infrastructure of machine readable documents application. Because travel documents and especially e-passports are the most discussed application of machine readable documents within the scientific community, we concentrate on them in subsection 2.2 and on their security and privacy threats in subsection 2.3.

2.1   Techical Infrastructure

The main components of an RFID enabled machine readable document application are the document itself, the reader device, the reader's control and crypto unit and an online database. These components and their mutual communication channels are illustrated in Figure 1. The document is a physical entity that contains an integrated RFID transponder that serves as a contactless memory device. Typically the transponder stores at least a unique identifier (UID) number. In addition, the transponder can provide logical functionalities like access control (through key comparison), random number generation and data encryption. Thus, the transponder serves as more than a mere barcode label.

The two-way communication in the air interface between the contactless memory device and the reader is indicated as a two directional arrow in Figure 1. Without specific addressing, RFID air interface is not secure and the transponder is vulnerable to clandestine scanning (or *skimming*) and eavesdropping. These two security threats are denoted as dashed lines in the illustration. A commonly used standard for RFID air interface of machine readable documents like e-passports is the ISO 14443 for proximity cards.

The reader device is responsible of the wireless communication. It is connected to the control and crypto unit through a closed, secure channel. Last component in the general infrastructure is the online database that represents data on the network. Though this database is not used in the proposed approaches, it is presented to complete the general view.

2.2   Travel Documents

Machine readable travel documents (MRTD) comprise e-passports, visas and special purpose ID/border-crossing cards [8]. Because of their similar nature, we include also driver's licenses within this group. Most public discussion around MRTDs has been around the electronic passports. The first e-passports were

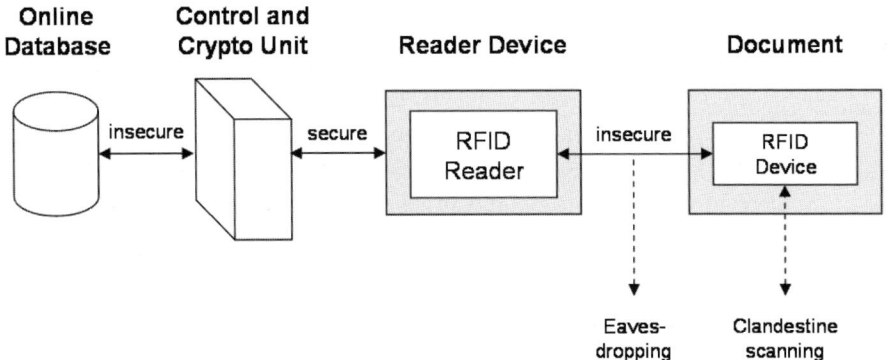

Fig. 1. Technical infrastructure and communication channels of RFID enabled machine readable documents. Security threats of eavesdropping and clandestine scanning are illustrated with dashed lines.

issued in 1998 by Malaysia, followed by other early adopters [5]. The Malaysian e-passports use an RFID transponder to store a fingerprint image of the passport's holder, which enables automated border checks with less human oversight. E-passports will be a prominent and widespread form of identification within a couple of years [16] as its adaptation is fueled for example by the U.S. Visa-Waiver Program [20] that involves twenty-seven nations. Not all MRTDs of today use RFID technology. Currently the vast majority of U.S. states use or have plans to use 2-D barcodes to store personal data on driver's licenses [4].

The role of the digital memory devices in the authentication processes of travel documents is twofold: on the one hand they help authenticating the traveler and on the other hand they help proving the authenticity of the document itself. Current e-passport (de-facto) standards are given by the ICAO guidelines [8]. They define only one mandatory security measure that is digital signature. Verifying the integrity of biometric features is of primary importance for passports, but addressing only data integrity leaves the system open to various security and privacy threats. The ICAO guidelines do define other cryptographic features that make use of public-key infrastructure, but these are optional.

E-Passport design has to address needs for individual privacy and national security and thus it poses severe security and privacy requirements. These requirements are discussed in [16] and [9]. First of all, the integrity and authenticity of the data the passport stores has to be guaranteed. Second, the data has to be kept confidential from non-authorized parties. Third, the passport must not pose privacy threats for its carrier and, furthermore, all these have to be fulfilled in a public system during up to 10 year long life-span of the passport.

2.3 Security and Privacy Threats

Most discussion about security and privacy of machine readable documents comes from the field of e-passports. Because of their rigid security requirements listed in subsection 2.2, also we concentrate on e-passports in order to provide a short overview of common security threats of machine readable documents in general.

Juels et al. [16] have discussed the security issues of e-passports and the following four threats, among others, were brought into light: clandestine scanning, clandestine tracking, eavesdropping, and cryptographic weaknesses. Moreover, the authors concluded that the e-passports do not provide sufficient protection for their biometric data. Threats do not only concern the functionality of the system but the security and privacy of its users as well. Also Pattison [21] has listed his concerns about the security of e-passports, concerning the baseline ICAO guidelines. These concerns comprise: unprotected data, unprotected wireless transmission, and missing connection between the chip and the paper. The last of these concerns is relevant regarding forgery because without this connection, the system can be fooled for example by putting a valid transponder into a fake paper.

The security of e-passports clearly needs careful addressing - compromising the system would threaten individual and national security. The U.S. State Department has already altered its e-passport design due to privacy concerns [26]. Various proposals for addressing the security and privacy issues of RFID do exist, most often based authentication protocols that use public or symmetric key encryption [2, 18, 9]. Scarce resources on the chip limit the use of cryptographic primitives and the goal of the design is often low-cost low-security features.

In the following section we present how optical memory devices can be combined with RFID to overcome some of the security threats of machine readable documents. The addressed security issues comprise:

- No connection between chip and paper
- Data integrity
- Clandestine scanning
- Clandestine tracking
- Eavesdropping

The first two aforementioned issues relate to the security of the overall system and the latter three to the unsecured wireless communication.

3   Combining RFID and Optical Memory Devices

We propose integrating an optical memory device into the RFID enabled machine readable document. What is common to all optical memory devices is that they need a line of sight connection for reading, making them resistant against clandestine reading and eavesdropping. Therefore we can assume that this channel is secure. The optical memory devices we refer to work normally with write-once-read-many (WORM) principle. Figure 2 illustrates how the addition of optical memory device extends the communication channels between machine readable document and reader device.

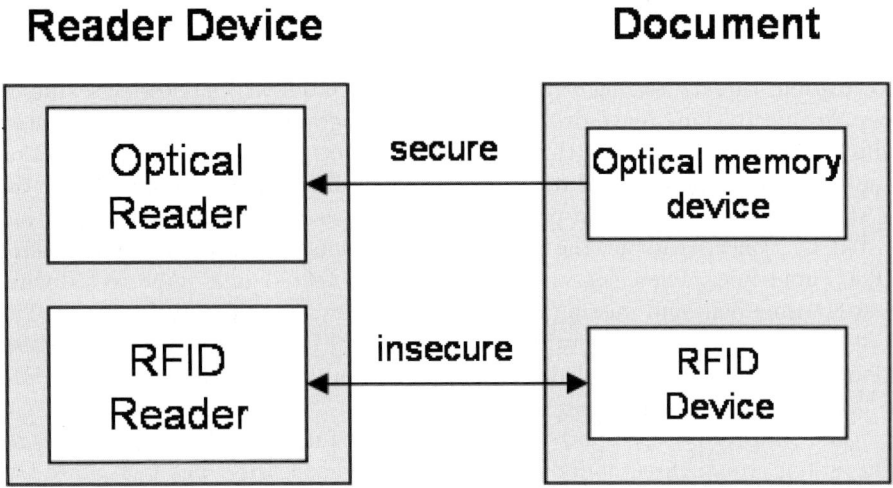

Fig. 2. The communication channels between reader device and document using RFID and optical memory.

Before we present our approaches, a short introduction to optical memory devices is provided. Even though we do specify what types of memory devices should be used, basic understanding of possible technologies is necessary for the following discussion.

3.1   Optical Memory Devices

Optical memory device refers to numerous technologies, ranging from barcodes to holographic memories with storage capacities on the order of 1 byte to 100 GB, respectively. The optical memory devices are characterized by their data density (e.g. bytes/mm2) and can support for error correction coding so that data from partially damaged devices can be successfully recovered. The reader or scanner devices of optical memories use photo sensors, laser and charge-coupled devices (CCD). One interesting advantage of optical memory devices, concerning especially printed codes, is that they are easy to integrate in documents in a rather permanent way as the ink that makes the code is inside the paper. Permanent integration of the memory device is important because it contributes to the security of the overall document.

The simplest low capacity optical memory devices are printed one and two dimensional barcodes. Memory capacities of typical barcodes vary from 95 bits of EAN.UCC-12 barcode to maximum data density of about 850 bits per cm2 of PDF-417 2-D code. In general, the maximum memory capacity of 2-D barcodes is defined by the accuracy of printing and scanning and the redundancy of the code. The printed high-density 2-D codes can provide data capacities up to about 1,250 KB per cm2 [10].

Holograms and holographic memory form another type of optical memory devices. Since the early seventies, it has been seen as the high capacity storage solution of the future, promising data densities on the order of hundreds of megabytes per square centimeter and remarkable improvements to the data transfer rate [29]. Hologram based optical memory devices are currently being used for example as anti-counterfeiting labels [1]. Also other promising optical memory technologies emerge, for example photoaddressable polymers (PAPs) which offer re-writeable (RW) data storage capabilities [6]. PAPs are promising recording materials for optical data storage applications such as high-capacity DVDs and holographic memory.

In the following subsections we present four approaches how the combination of RFID and optical memory devices can be used to increase the security of machine readable documents. First two approaches address data integrity and bind the chip and the document, while the two other approaches aim at securing the communication. For the sake of simplicity, we use the term reader in the rest of this paper for the combination of optical and RFID reader devices and their control and crypto unit. Because machine readable documents often relate to a physical entity, we assume that data of interest that the document stores relates to this entity. We denote this data as *object specific data* and it can be used for example in authentication. In addition, the documents can store any other application specific data which is merely referred to as *other data*. This other data can be static or dynamic.

3.2   Storing the Object Specific Data in the Optical Memory

In this basic approach, the static object specific data is stored on both the RFID transponder and on the optical memory. This is illustrated in Figure 3. Mirroring the data of interest helps to maintain redundancy and thus increases the reliability of the overall document. Redundancies on other media than contactless memory devices may be important as the electronic devices can be destroyed without visual effect. Moreover, the additional use of optical storage devices may help overcoming problems resulting from limited storage capacities of RFID devices.

The advantage of mirroring the data is to have a mechanism - indicated by the *resul* block in Figure 3 - that can tell if one of the two devices has been tampered with. This increases the integrity of the data, though an identical tampering of both devices cannot be detected. In addition, the object or person specific data also interlinks the two devices in an unquestionable way, since this data can be used as a unique identifier of the physical entity. A disadvantage of this approach is that a relatively large size optical memory is needed. Furthermore, the optical

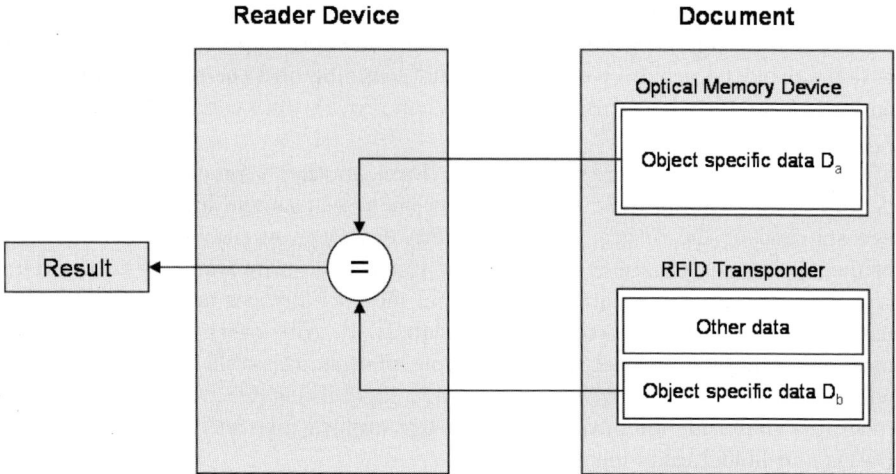

Fig. 3. An illustration of storing the object specific data in the optical memory device.

memory doesn't provide access control and thus offers another medium where the data is vulnerable to skimming.

3.3   Storing Hash of the Object Specific Data in Optical Memory

The basic step for taking advantage of the additional data integrity and bind between paper and chip of the first approach while guarding the object specific data from optical access is to save only a hash value of the data on the optical device. This comes with the expense of some extra computations and losing the optical backup of the data of interest. The data structures of the memory devices and the data integrity check of the document using this approach are illustrated in Figure 4.

The used hash function needs to be known by the party performing the data integrity check so the specification of the hash function is stored on the chip. Moreover, this gives an additional binding between the two storage devices. Including the transponder UID number in the hash-calculation can also strengthen this linkage. The reader has to calculate the hash value of the object specific data loaded from the contactless device in order to perform the integrity check. Compared to the previous approach, another advantage of storing the hash value is that smaller optical storage space is needed.

3.4   Storing Access Keys in the Optical Memory

While the two previous approaches in subsections 3.2 and 3.3 define data integrity checks, this approach aims at protecting the data. In this approach the RFID transponder does not reveal the object specific data if no correct access

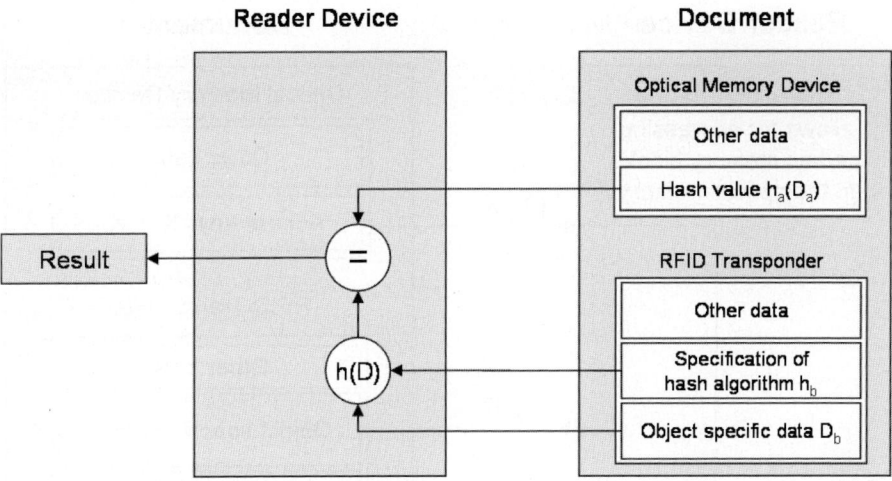

Fig. 4. An illustration of storing hash of the object specific data in the optical memory device.

key (e.g. a PIN code) has been transmitted in advance, which prevents clandestine reading. Moreover, the data on the electronic tag is read-protected. Also the emission of transponder serial number can be protected in the way described above, protecting the document and its bearer against clandestine tracking. The access key is stored on the optical device and thus can only be read with a line of sight connection. In the context of e-passports, for example, this means that the passport has to be opened for reading and therefore its owner can control who can have access to the contactless memory.

Figure 5 illustrates how the reader can access the object specific data using this approach. Now the requirements of the tag include an access control unit which is capable of generating random indexes and comparing keys. The communication model works as follows: The RFID reader initiates the session by asking the transponder for an index i between 1 and N, where N indicates the number of access keys stored in the document. For the sake of simplicity, this message is not illustrated is Figure 5. After the index value is transmitted by the transponder, the reader can obtain the corresponding key K_i from the optical memory and send it to the RFID transponder. We denote the length of K_i as M (bits). The transponder access control unit verifies if the received access key matches the one stored in its memory and can grant the access for the reader.

In this approach the link between the paper and transponder is strong and both optical and contactless devices are needed for successful communication. In order to access the object specific data, an attacker has to obtain or successfully guess the access key that matches the requested one. Because single access keys can be still obtained by eavesdropping the radio channel between the reader and the transponder, the number of access keys N needs to be large enough to make the malicious use of compromised keys infeasible and spoofing access keys

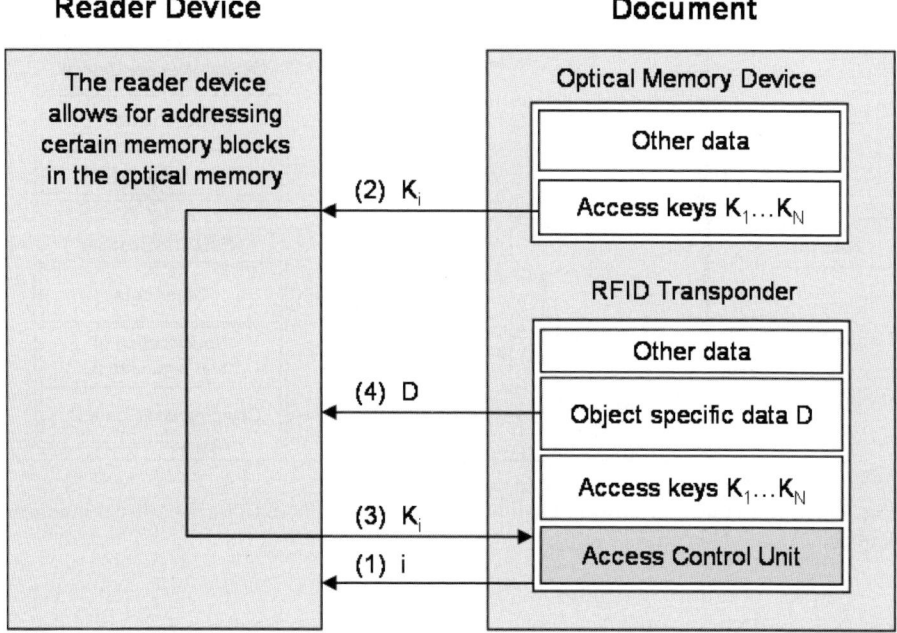

Fig. 5. An illustration of storing access keys in the optical memory device.

difficult. More precisely, N should be chosen in such a way that the probability of getting access with a compromised key in a single random challenge, $Pr = \frac{1}{N}$, is not significantly greater than the probability of guessing an access key, $Pr = 2^{-M}$.

Spoofing access keys can be also countered by temporarily locking the tag when anyone tries to unlock it using a false access key. However, we leave this to be addressed by the more detailed level protocol design.

3.5   Storing Session Keys in the Optical Memory

This fourth approach is similar to the previous one presented in subsection 3.4 where the transponder challenges the reader for a response to be read from the optical device. However, instead of using access keys which can be eavesdropped from the reader-to-tag radio channel, in this approach the optical memory device stores session keys that are used to encrypt the communication.

How the combination of RFID and optical memory is used for protecting the communication in this approach is illustrated in Figure 6. The access control is established by a challenge response pair which is initiated by the tag by transmitting a pseudo-random challenge ch and an index i between 1 and N. After having received the index, the reader accesses the optical memory of the document to obtain the corresponding session key K_i. To authenticate itself to the transponder, the reader calculates and sends the response *resp* which is the challenge encrypted using the session key, denoted by $K_i(ch)$ in Figure 6. Last, the session key K_i is used to encrypt the following wireless communication (e.g. transmission of the object specific data) which takes place between the reader and the transponder, to provide protection against eavesdropping.

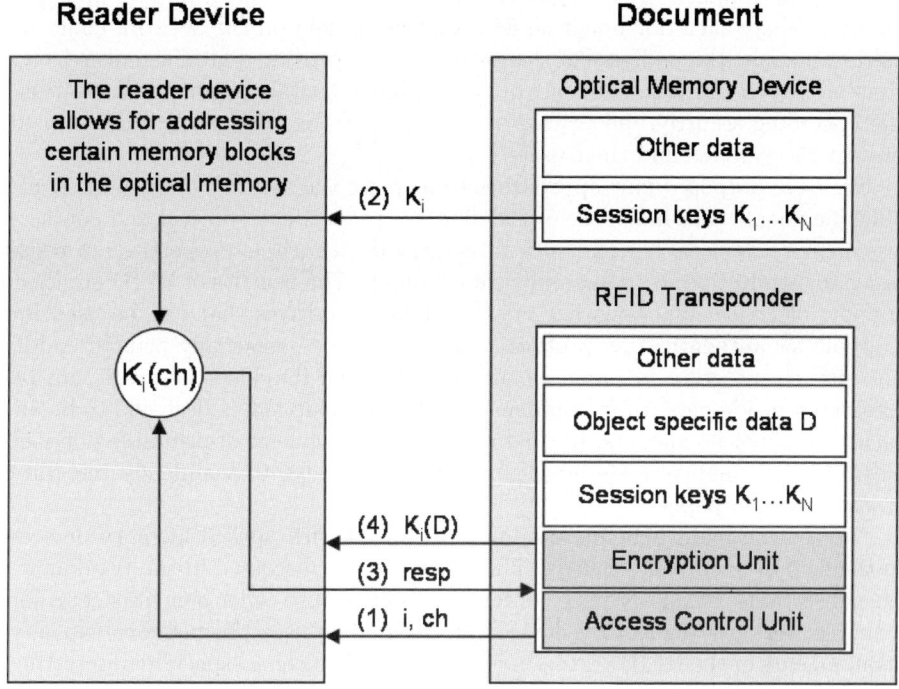

Fig. 6. An illustration of storing session keys in the optical memory device.

In this approach the successful authentication means that the reader has optical access to the document. Storing session keys in the optical device provides comparable benefits than the approach in subsection 3.4 where access keys are stored on the optical device. Most notably, the passport has to be opened for reading and the two storage media provide strong interlink between the devices. In addition, the use of session keys and encryption provides protection against eavesdropping. Most importantly, the session key is never transmitted in the insecure radio channel as this key is only optically accessible, which overcomes the weakness of the previous approach regarding compromised access keys. On the other hand, this approach requires the transponder to support data encryption.

The presented design has still cryptographic weakness regarding the use of session keys. These keys are not chosen in a truly random manner but taken from a restricted list which makes the authentication protocol more vulnerable for attacks. Nevertheless, even the use of only one session key ($N = 1$) provides good protection for the machine readable document.

4   Discussion

Providing machines with the capability to communicate with documents through RFID could dramatically change the way we see and use them: besides precisely knowing where each document is, data on the tag and on the network could be used to manage the pedigree of the documents, to provide digital signatures etc. However, when the documents are of great value or contain personal information, the upcoming security and privacy threats need to be adequately addressed to protect the systems and their users.

We have proposed four approaches to increase the security of machine readable documents that make use of the different properties of optical and contactless memory devices. For the optical memory device, these properties are resistance to clandestine scanning and eavesdropping. The benefits of RFID are their support of logical functions like cryptographic primitives that can be used for example for authentication protocols. Optical devices, especially printed codes, are easy to integrate in paper documents. Also RFID chips, however, can be integrated inside paper; for example the Hitachi μ-chip [24] is designed to be attached to paper documents. In the future, the development of printable polymer electronics [7] may provide novel and interesting ways to seamlessly integrate transponders in paper.

We see the main benefits of combining RFID with optical memory devices in the field of document security. These benefits are discussed in the two following subsections. Besides strengthening the security, also other benefits occur, for example the optical memory device can be used to ease the memory capacity requirements of the RFID transponder. This might become especially interesting in the future with the radical data capacity improvements of emerging optical memory technologies. Furthermore, the optical memory device on the document gives a visual cue of the existence of the tag for the users and holders of the document, which can contribute for the acceptance of RFID technology in general.

4.1   Increased Communication Security

The optical channel can be used to overcome threats relating clandestine scanning and eavesdropping in ways presented in subsections 3.4 and 3.5. These approaches require no pre-distribution of shared secrets between the reader and the document, which favors for simpler systems; indeed, key distribution is seen as one of the future challenges of RFID security [14]. On the other hand no mutual authentication between the devises is provided. Here the security is established by the assumption that a party who has free visual access to the document is trusted - an assumption that we consider quite feasible regarding for example passports, because, tagged or not, they are to be kept safe and presented to authorized personnel only.

In any case, especially concerning public systems, high level of security needs to be established through secret keys. The presented approaches do not limit the use of public or symmetric key cryptography and so they can be used inside the communication models. Furthermore, the proposed approaches can be combined with each other, namely by selecting one of the first two approaches (subsections 3.2 and 3.3) to guarantee the data integrity and one of the latter two approaches (subsections 3.4 and 3.5) to secure the communication, while taking into account the hardware constraints of reader and memory devices.

With regard to the security and privacy threats of e-passports listed in subsection 2.3, the increased communication security of the approaches presented in subsections 3.4 and 3.5 would help overcome concerns about clandestine scanning, clandestine tracking and eavesdropping.

4.2   Increased Security of the Overall System

Other security contributions of the proposed approaches include increased data integrity, as presented in subsections 3.1 and 3.2. Also a strong bind between the paper and the chip is provided, which answers to the e-passport security concern of missing connection between the paper and the tag, as discussed in subsection 2.3.

The use of two memory devices adds complexity to the system and thus makes the documents harder to be cloned or forged. Even though this conflicts the fundamental security doctrine of Kerckhoffs which says that the security of a system should depend on its key, not on its design obscurity [19], it can provide effective ways to combat counterfeits. For example, the approaches allow for selection of a proprietary optical memory type which cannot be read using devices that are publicly available, if a closed-loop application is preferred.

Also the link between the paper and the tag contributes to cloning resistance: Tags can be made hard to clone by using read protected memories or factory programmed unique transponder ID numbers. An example of how the read protected KILL password of EPCglobal Class-1 Generation-2 tags [3] can be used to strengthen the transponder against cloning can be found in [15]. In addition, special efforts have been made towards anti-clone tags [27]. Consequently, when the seamlessly integrated optical memory device binds the document to an anti-clone tag, cloning and forging the document becomes even harder.

4.3   Related Work

The potential of RFID to secure physical documents is well established. Takaragi et al. [24] have discussed how to prevent forgery of security papers by integrating small RFID tags into the physical documents. The authors compared RFID to barcode and concluded that RFID provides better counterfeit protection due to the fact that it is harder to be copied. However, no link (expect for the physical integration) between the transponder and the document was provided.

The optical channel can be used in RFID also in other ways. Raskar et al. [22] have developed photosensing wireless tags called radio frequency identification and geometry (RFIG) transponders that support for geometric functions. Making use of the photo-sensors, RFIG allows for tags being read only when properly illuminated, which could be used to solve the problem of clandestine scanning of machine readable documents. However, on the contrary to our approaches, no information is transferred in RFIG from the transponder to the reader through this optical channel and, furthermore, no optical memory devices were used. Because of these two facts, our approaches have more potential to increase the security of machine readable documents.

Combining RFID with data printed on the object is not novel in security applications and it has been used for example for privacy protection of tagged banknotes [17]. In this approach the printed serial number (and a signature value) of the banknote is read, namely using OCR, and used to bind the banknote and its RFID chip. Printed data is also being used for the security of travel documents in the advanced security methods defined by optional ICAO e-passport guidelines [9]. In the so called basic access control protocol the e-passport has to be opened and clear-text data like passport number and data of birth of the bearer is used to derive secret cryptographic keys. The purpose of this protocol is to prevent skimming and eavesdropping but according to [16] the scheme fails due to too small entropy of the keys and the fact that only one key is provided for the lifetime of the passport.

This review shows that the previously proposed approaches differ from the contribution of this paper in the way that we make use of the secure optical channel from the document to the reader that cannot be eavesdropped. Furthermore, the existing approaches that use machine readable optical data on documents are normally based on OCR of printed clear-text data, whereas we propose using dedicated optical memory devices which support for much larger storage spaces.

5   Conclusions

In this paper we have shown different approaches to combine RFID and optical memory devices in order to increase the security of machine readable documents. In particular, we have presented how the proposed approaches could overcome existing security threats of electronic passports concerning eavesdropping and clandestine scanning and tracking. Instead of establishing security based on sharing secrets between the reader device and the document before the communication, we make use of the optical channel between the document and the reader which cannot be read or eavesdropped without a line of sight. Even though strong security in communications always needs secret keys, security of RFID enabled machine readable documents will also depend on a strong connection between the transponder and the paper. We have illustrated how optical memory devices can be used to provide this connection. In conclusion, we believe that the interlinked co-existence of RFID and optical memory devices can play an important role for strengthening the security of smart documents of the future.

References

1. Tesa AG. Protection system by Tesa Scribos marks spare part packs.
   http://www.tesa.com/corporate/211628.html (28.3.2006), 2006.
2. T. Dimitriou. A lightweight RFID protocol to protect against traceability and cloning attacks. In *Conference on Security and Privacy for Emerging Areas in Communication Networks – SecureComm*, Athens, Greece, September 2005. IEEE.
3. EPCglobal. Class-1 generation-2 UHF RFID conformance requirements specification v. 1.0.2. EPCglobal public document, October 4, 2005.
4. American Association for Motor Vehicle Administrators. Current and planned technologies for U.S. jurisdictions.
   http://www.aamva.org/standards/stdUSLicenseTech.asp (22.3.2006), 2006.
5. RFID Gazette. E-passports. News article, November 8, 2005.
   http://www.rfidgazette.org/airline/index.html (28.3.2006), 2005.
6. R. Hagen and T. Bieringer. Photoaddressable polymers for optical data storage. Advanced Materials Volume 13, Issue 23, Pages 1805 - 1810, 2001.
7. C. Hammerschmidt. Polymer electronics yet to realize promise. EETimes Germany, November 2004.
8. ICAO. Document 9303, machine readable travel documents.
   http://www.icao.int/mrtd/publications/doc.cfm (28.3.2006), October 2004.
9. ICAO. PKI for machine readable travel documents offering icc read-only access, technical report, version 1.1. http://www.icao.int/mrtd/publications/doc.cfm (28.3.2006), October 2004.
10. Veritec Inc. VSCode technology overview.
    http://www.veritecinc.com/vs_code.html (28.3.2006), 2006.
11. RFID Journal. U.S. tests e-passports. News Article, November 2, 2004.
12. RFID Journal. United states sets date for e-passports. News Article, October 25, 2005.
13. RFID Journal. Roman lab to offer commercial services. News Article, March 28, 2006.
14. A. Juels. RFID security and privacy: A research survey. Manuscript, September 2005.
15. A. Juels. Strengthening EPC tags against cloning. Manuscript, March 2005.
16. A. Juels, D. Molnar, and D. Wagner. Security and privacy issues in e-passports. In *Conference on Security and Privacy for Emerging Areas in Communication Networks – SecureComm*, Athens, Greece, September 2005. IEEE.
17. A. Juels and R. Pappu. Squealing euros: Privacy protection in RFID-enabled banknotes. In Rebecca N. Wright, editor, *Financial Cryptography – FC'03*, volume 2742 of *Lecture Notes in Computer Science*, pages 103–121, Le Gosier, Guadeloupe, French West Indies, January 2003. IFCA, Springer-Verlag.
18. A. Juels and S. Weis. Authenticating pervasive devices with human protocols. In Victor Shoup, editor, *Advances in Cryptology – CRYPTO'05*, volume 3126 of *Lecture Notes in Computer Science*, pages 293–308, Santa Barbara, California, USA, August 2005. IACR, Springer-Verlag.
19. A. Kerckhoffs. La cryptographie militaire.
    http://www.petitcolas.net/fabien/kerckhoffs/ (21.4.2006), January 1883.
20. U.S. Department of State. Visa-waiver program (VWP).
    http://travel.state.gov/visa/temp/without/without_1990.html (20.4.2006), 2006.
21. N. Pattison. Securing and enhancing the privacy of the e-passport with contactless electronic chips. Contact: pattison@axalto.com, 2005.

22. R. Raskar, P. Beardsley, J. Baar, Y. Wang, P.H. Dietz, J. Lee, D. Leigh, and T. Willwacher. RFIG lamps: Interacting with a self-describing world via photosensing wireless tags and projectors. *ACM Transactions on Graphics (TOG) SIGGRAPH*, 23(3):406–415, August 2004.
23. T. Staake, F. Thiesse, and E. Fleisch. Extending the EPC network - the potential of RFID in anti-counterfeiting. In *2005 ACM symposium on Applied computing*, pages 1607–1612, New York (NY), 2005. ACM Press.
24. K. Takaragi, M. Usami, R. Imura, and T. Itsuki, R. andSatoh. An ultra small individual recognition security chip. IEEE Micro, November-December, 2001.
25. C. Tellkamp, A. Angerer, E. Fleisch, and D. Corsten. From pallet to shelf: Improving data quality in retail supply chains using rfid. Cutter IT Journal - The Journal of Information Technology Management, Vol. 17, No. 9, pp. 19-24, 2004.
26. International Herald Tribune. U.S. to alter passport design because of privacy fears. News Article, April 28, 2005.
27. P. Tuyls and L. Batina. Rfid-tags for anti-counterfeiting. In David Pointcheval, editor, *Topics in Cryptology - CT-RSA 2006, The Cryptographers' Track at the RSA Conference 2006*, Lecture Notes in Computer Science, San Jose, CA, USA, February 2006. Springer-Verlag.
28. S. Weis. Rfid privacy workshop: Concerns, consensus, and questions. IEEE Security and Privacy, vol. 02, no. 2, pp. 48-50, 2004.
29. M.J. Wickett. Memories of the future. emerging replacements for semiconductor memory, optical and magnetic disks. Multimedia Systems - MMS 2002, South Hampton, UK, January 2002, 2002.
30. K. Wong, P. Hui, and A. Chan. Cryptography and authentication on RFID passive tags for apparel products. *Computers in Industry*, May 2006.

Accessing Ambient Intelligence through Devices with Low Computational and Communication Power

Franco Borello[1], Dario Bonino[2], and Fulvio Corno[2]

[1] Progetto Lagrange - Fondazione CRT, c/o Politecnico di Torino, Torino, Italy
borello@cad.polito.it
[2] Politecnico di Torino, Torino, Italy {fulvio.corno, dario.bonino}@polito.it

Abstract. This paper presents an architecture allowing simple access to Ambient Intelligent Systems deployed in domestic environments. Interaction can be performed through a wide range of devices, from traditional PCs to laptops, mobile phones, digital television sets, and so on. Particular focus is devoted to low computational power devices, which are the main target of the proposed approach. These devices are seen as simple terminal interfaces that remotely communicate with the home environment, by means of a so-called Interaction Manager. A user-interface application for the digital television Set-Top Box shows the feasibility of the approach and poses the basis for further works in the pro-posed direction.

1 Introduction

Ambient Intelligence is a rather new research field that refers to smart electronic environments that can enhance several aspects of people life. It aims at achieving human-centric computing by making environments more intelligent and by adopting interface technologies that provide natural, multi-modal interaction, credible to the human brain [1]. In a domestic environment, ambient intelligence is often materialized in the concept of smart home or domotic-system. Such a concept can be variously designed and implemented, as many are the possible ways to improve the home environment through automation and intelligent behaviors. Diverse are also the devices used for controlling the household intelligence, including personal computers, PDAs or mobile phones. These devices can be felt "friendly" by many technologically aware people, but they can result obtrusive and difficult to use for some users categories, elderly and disabled people for example. Too technological interfaces can, in other words, become a sensible barrier to the users for exploiting the benefits of smart homes. In order to solve this problem, user interaction with the domestic environment shall be based on devices that already occupy a relevant place in the everyday life of final users, the television being the more evident example. Using the television as interface for domotic environments is nowadays feasible, and economically convincing thanks to the increasing spread of the digital terrestrial television technology (DVB-T

[2]) in Europe, and in Italy particularly. The driving technology object is the so-called decoder (or Set-Top-Box, STB), which often offers several facilities for managing multimedia and interactive interfaces (being based on MHP [3]). The Set-Top Box has enough intelligence on-board to manage TV-like interfaces (mainly text-based) and therefore to manage similar interfaces for controlling the house devices. However, since the computational power of the STB is fairly limited, it cannot manage the entire logic of a control application. As a consequence, the interface level of a hypothetic control software can be effectively managed by the STB while the application level must be kept separated, on a more powerful machine, a PC as an example. Separating the interface logic from the application logic is not a new solution. According to several Human-Computer Interaction studies applications running on a given hardware platform must be independent from the devices and methods used for human-computer interaction. This allows interface designers to develop interfaces adapted to the needs and peculiarities of the user (and to the features of the user access device) without modifying the application. Independence between applications and interfaces becomes even crucial when design is focused on users with disabilities. Due to the great diversity of their impairments, in fact, a wide range of different interfaces is needed [4]. This paper presents an interaction architecture that allows controlling different domotic networks and domestic appliances through a plurality of user access devices, with a particular attention to devices with reduced communication and elaboration capacity. The architecture has been designed and developed in the context of a collaboration with the CRIT RAI [5] research center, having as goal the design and development of innovative, user-centered applications for the Set Top Box technology. A digital television application has been developed, on top of the proposed architecture, which allows controlling a smart home equipped with a MyHome BTicino domotic network [6], through the TV remote control. Thanks to the House Manager concept already developed by some of the authors [7], the same application can also be used to control devices not connected with the BTicino network, a music server, in the provided scenario. The innovative points include the capability of separating the house control interface from the house control logic, thus allowing to access the domotic network through much more devices than usual, including television, cell-phones, lap-tops, PCs, palm-tops, etc. and the capability of interfacing many domotic networks and appliances through a single, accessible, interface application. The paper is organized as follows: Section 2 introduces the design principles on which the platform has been built and the resulting architecture. Section 3 describes the testing environment and the TV-based interface while Section 4 presents experimental results. Eventually Section 5 draws conclusions and proposes some future works.

2   Architecture

In this section an overview of the proposed logical architecture (Figure 1) is presented, followed by a more detailed description of each involved component.

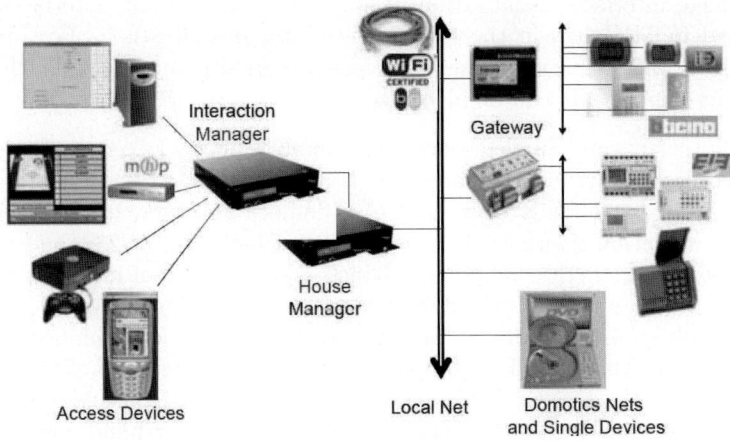

Fig. 1. The proposed Logical Architecture.

As briefly discussed in the introduction, the STB has not sufficient computational power to manage the entire logic of house control applications. So, the
interface layer and the application logic must be separated and the latter shall
be executed by more powerful systems such as a PC or a Home Gateway. In
the proposed architecture the "elaboration" centre for the interface generation
and for the management of the application logic is the "Interaction manager".
Instead, interaction with house components, i.e., abstraction of low-level legacy
protocols and access technologies to a common, TCP-based, communication protocol is delegated to the House Manager. User devices are considered as simple
terminals. This allows to design and deploy a device-independent interaction architecture as no assumptions are taken about the device capabilities. The access
elements must only be able to show the information elements delivered by the
Interaction Manager and to gather user choices, keys pressed or items selected,
sending them back to the Manager. For several aspects this solution resembles
some already published thin-client models [8], but it is different both in gener-
ality and scope. While thin clients aim at subdividing the "heavy" computation
of applications from the more lightweight interface management, the proposed
approach aims at completely removing the interface logic from the terminal
thus allowing the execution on very limited clients. In addition, thin clients are
usually supported by general frameworks able to wrap many different applications and to convert them into couples of lightweight interfaces and computation
back-ends. The proposed system, instead is strictly devoted to house-control applications, and by no means needs to be as general as thin client platforms. This
major specialization allows, on the contrary, the architecture to be more open
to different devices and technologies as the terminals must only implement the

correct communication protocol and offer the proper functionalities, while they can manage interface visualization in autonomy. As a result, interfaces can be developed in MHP (as in the experiments later described), in Java, in C++, Symbian, J2ME, etc. By looking at the general architecture shown in (Figure 1) four main components can be identified:

- Domotic Nets and Single Devices: The domotic networks "controllable" through the proposed architecture and the devices distributed in the environment, which are not already connected to a domotic network, but that possess a communication interface (Ethernet, WiFi, Bluetooth, RS232, and so on);
- House Manager: the component, which is responsible of interfacing the domotic nets and the single devices and of abstracting the low-level legacy protocols spoken by each of them to a common, high level, unified language;
- Interaction Manager: The computationally strong front-end of the proposed interaction framework that, communicating with the House Manager on one hand and with the user's Access Device on the other hand, empowers the user interface generation and management. It is accessible by many kinds of Access Devices, through a proper communication protocol;
- Access Devices: computationally poor devices, which provide visualization of the graphical user interface and transmit the user's choices to the Interaction Manager, acting as simple terminals.

2.1   Domotic Nets and Single Devices

In a domestic environment several domotic networks can be deployed, each produced by different manufacturers. They can be composed of many devices distributed into the domestic ambient, and connected to each other by means of a "domotic" bus. Devices exchange information and commands through this bus, using a well-defined protocol that is specific for each domotic technology (EIB, BTicino, etc.). A branded domotic network can be accessed from outside the network by means of a device called "gateway". The gateway communicates on one side with the domotic network and on the other side with external devices (a PC for example) through a LAN connection, possibly using a different protocol. The domestic environment also includes single devices, i.e., devices which would not natively cooperate in the same bus-based environment, but that can be accessed by a PC using a serial port, a USB port or other.

2.2   House Manager

The House Manager is a concept developed by the e-Lite group of the Politecnico di Torino and presented at SAC 2006 [7]. Its structure (Figure 2) derives from standard house gateways being actively studied in the last years. The most interesting features, are the capability to "abstract" the home functionalities using a high-level common language and the rule-based intelligence layer.

The manager architecture, can be roughly subdivided in an abstraction layer and an intelligence layer. The abstraction layer, which includes the communication layer, the device drivers and the controlled devices/environments provides

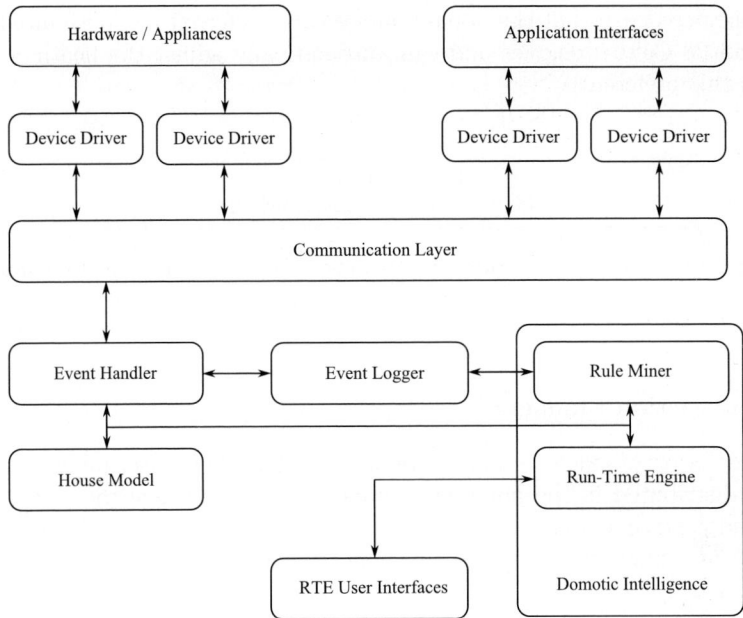

Fig. 2. The House Manager internal architecture.

means for translating low level bus protocols into a common, high-level, human readable protocol that allows to uniformly access every domotic network and every home device, in a transparent manner. Such a protocol adopts a URI-like notation for devices and a predefined set of commands associated to each device type (see Figure 3 for some examples). This ensures, from one side the ability to virtually control all "electrically controllable" devices of a given household, and on the other side the ability to deploy the proposed system in different environments, with different settings, granting the desired accessibility level, at the hard-ware abstraction layer, at least.

The intelligence layer is composed by the modules that in (Figure 2) lie below the communication layer. These modules allow to access domestic devices using an interaction model similar to that of human beings. The House Model for example, provides notions such as neighbourhood between controllable devices and furniture elements, abstraction of functional types of devices, etc. Using this model a user may issue a command like "shut down the light near the armchair in my bed room", or can issue a "light-up" command to a dimmer-driven light which usually has only continue values of lighting that can range from 0 to 100%. The House Model is complemented by the Rule-Miner and the Rule-Engine that add some automated behavior to the Manager either by learning rules from user behaviors or by executing predefined rules. So, for example, one can set up a rule for blinking the light of the room in which he/she is located when the fridge gets switched off, so that he/she can avoid foods to deteriorate. In another case, the house may learn that the home temperature preferred by house inhabitants is around 20 Celsius degrees and can automatically adjust the heating system to meet this preference.

```
kitchen.light.ON
lounge.cdplayer.play(track=2)
```

Fig. 3. The URI-like notation for accessing devices and their functionalities.

2.3   Interaction Manager

The Interaction Manager is a Java application that allows user interaction with devices distributed in the home environment. It can manage the usual direct-command pattern as well as more complex scenarios and alarms. A scenario is a sequence of commands associated to a single menu item; an alarm can be raised by a particular status of a device, the fridge off in the former example. The inter-action manager basically acts as an interface proxy: on one side communicates with the House Manager, using a unified high-level protocol on an XML-RPC transport layer. On the other side it manages the workflow of the entire control application and interacts with access devices for updating the graphical inter-faces shown to the user and for gathering user actions. The Interaction Manager can operate many concurrent access devices as follows. For each of them it gen-erates the user interface content, while the access device allocates and disposes the areas for the content to be displayed. Then, it sends to the access device the interface "pages", the content of each page and the references to the interface areas in which the same content shall be allocated. Once the access device has displayed the page, it notifies the Interaction Manager which then sends the proper updating information (change of devices status, status messages, etc.) at every time it is needed. When the user selects a interface element, the ac-cess device notifies the Interaction Manager which takes the proper actions and possibly requires the access device to change some elements of the currently dis-played interface. The Interaction Manager is configured by means of two XML configuration files: menu.xml and abstractLayouts.xml. The former defines the Manager internal configuration while the latter is used as template for building the configuration file of each access device.

AbstractLayout.xml (Figure 4) defines a "layout" list. A layout represents the structure of the graphical interface that the access devices propose to the user and is defined by a layout identifier and by a list of component identifiers.

Three types of components can be visualized on the user device display: informative items, interactive items and icons. An informative item represents a display area where the information to be provided to the user is shown, for example the page title area, a status message area, a tool tip message area. An interactive item is similar to an informative item, but in addition it is navigable

```
<ABSTRACT_LAYOUTS>
    <LAYOUT>
        <LAYOUT_ID>1<LAYOUT_ID>
            <INF_ITEM>
                <INF_ITEM_ID>TITLE</INF_ITEM_ID>
            <INF_ITEM>
            ...
            <INF_ITEM>
                <ITEM_ID>1</ITEM_ID>
            <INF_ITEM>
            ...
            <ICON>
                <ICON_ID>1</ICON_ID>
            </ICON>
            ...
    </LAYOUT>
<ABSTRACT_LAYOUTS>
```

Fig. 4. The structure of the abstractLayouts.xml file.

and is selectable by the user (a menu, for example). An icon item is defines the area where an icon representing a device status is shown. To better understand how each part of the abstractLayouts.xml works, it might be useful to analyze how layouts are loaded and displayed. When a new page of the user interface must be showed, the Interaction Manager sends to the access device a command for loading a new layout (Figure 5), including a valid layout identifier. The access device allocates then the areas for the component listed in the file abstract-Layouts.xml and associates to them the identifiers reported into the same file. Then the Interaction Manager requires to load the content of the single page components, sending, in addition, the item identifiers. A layout may contain a number of item greater than those contained in a given interface page thus supporting the reuse of the same layout for more than one page. However a layout must contain all the elements presents into the pages that use it.

Once generated the given interface, the Interaction Manager waits for connections from the client applications running on the Access Devices.

When a client application connects, the Interaction Manager creates a model of the various menus to be shown to the user, using the information stored in his configuration file, menu.xml. This file (shown in Figure 6) defines the menus to be visualized, as a page list. A layout identifier is associated to each page, which identifies, in the file abstractLayouts.xml, the layout with which the page shall be displayed. Pages are composed of several informative items, interactive items and devices to be monitored (for detecting alarms). Every item has a unique identifier, corresponding to the one reported in abstractLayouts.xml.

Returning to the process description, once the menu page has been displayed by the access device, every available interactive item can be selected by the user. If the interactive item is associated to a device, the action performed depends on

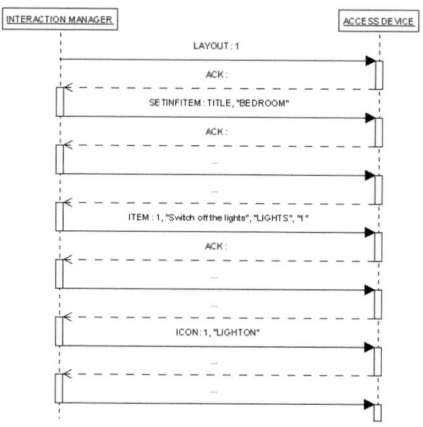

Fig. 5. The page-loading sequence diagram.

the status of the device. As a consequence, a given interactive item can trigger different actions associated to the possible statuses of the device it represents. Actions, in menu.xml, are defined by the following values:

- the device status (if needed),
- the name of the icon to be displayed when the status is reached (optional),
- the tool tip message associated the device status (indicating the operation to be performed if the item is selected),
- the text to be visualized in the item area (menu item)
- the command/s to be performed when the item is selected.

Communication protocol between the Interaction Manager and the Access Devices The Interaction Manager and the client process running on the user's Access Devices communicate through a custom protocol defined in the contest of this work, and transported over a proper TCP connection. Commands exchanged be-tween the two applications are strings of variable length, structured as reported below.

$$<STX>COMMAND<US>ARG\_1<US>...<US>ARG\_N<ETX>$$

Some escape sequences are used to delimit the commands and to separate the associated arguments. The command message starts with the delimiter character <STX>(ASCII code 2) while the inner elements are separated by the separator character <US>(decimal ASCII code 31). The whole string ends with the delimiter character <ETX>(ASCII code 3). The COMMAND place holder identifies the command type; ARG_1, ARG_N are, instead, information fields associated to the command. They can be present in a variable quantity, depending on the type of command. Communication between the Interaction Manager and access devices involves commands for page construction and users' choice notifications.

```
<MENU>
     <PAGE>
          <PAGE_ID>1</PAGE_ID>
          <LAYOUT_ID>1</LAYOUT_ID>
          <CHK_DEVICES_DISPLAY>TRUE</CHK_DEVICES_DISPLAY>
          <INF_ITEM>
               <INF_ITEM_ID>TITLE</INF_ITEM>
               <TEXT>BEDROOM </TEXT>
          </INF_ITEM>
          ...
          <INT_ITEM>
               <ITEM_ID>1</ITEM_ID>
               <TABORDER>1</TABORDER>
               <KEY>1</KEY>
               <ICON_ID>1</ICON_ID>
               <COMMANDS>
                    <CMD status="bedroom.lights.ON" icon_name="LIGHTON"
                    tooltip="Switch off the lights" description="LUCI"
                    command="bedroom.lights.OFF"/>
                    <CMD status="bedroom.lights.OFF" icon_name="LIGHTOFF"
                    tooltip="Switch on the lights" description="LUCI"
                    command="bedroom.lights.ON"/>
               </COMMANDS>
          </INT_ITEM>
          ...
     </PAGE>
     ...
     <CHECKED_DEVICE>
          <CHK_DEVICE_ID>1</CHK_DEVICE_ID>
          <INF_ITEM_ID>INFODEVICES</INF_ITEM_ID>
          <COMMANDS>
               <CMD status="bedroom.sensor.ON" text="Intrusion into bedroom"
               command="page.10"/>
               <CMD status="bedroom.sensor.OFF" text="Bedroom sensor re-setted"
               command="NONE"/>
               <CMD status="bedroom.sensor.RESET" text="Reset bedroom sensor"
               command="NONE"/>
          </COMMANDS>
     </CHECKED_DEVICE>
     ...
</MENU>
```

Fig. 6. An excerpt of the menu.xml file.

For example, the command string used for loading an informative item content (title, status message, etc.), is composed of the reserved word SETINFITEM followed by the element identifier and the text to be visualized:

<STX>SETINFITEM<US>INF_ITEM_ID<US>TEXT<ETX>

Communication from an access device to the Interaction Manager involves commands for communicating the user's choices and acknowledgements. For example, the command string used to communicate the user's selection of a rapid selection key is formed by the word KEY followed by the code of the key pressed:

<STX>KEY<US>KEY_CODE<ETX>

2.4   Access Devices

Access devices allow users to manage domestic appliances and automated components. A client application provides the visualization of the corresponding graphical user inter-face. While visualizing the user interface, the access device also acquires the user's choices sending them to the Interaction Manager. Communication between an Access Device and the Interaction Manager must respect the protocol introduced in section 2.4. Instead, the implementation of the various aspects involved by the client application is left to the programmer, first of all the choice of the programming language to adopt, which usually is imposed by the access device type. Client applications, once activated by the user, set-up a connection to the Interaction Manager, with a TCP socket, and wait for a layout loading command. When the Interaction Manager issues this command, the client application creates the graphical user interface structures, using its configuration file layouts.xml (Figure 7). This file is created by the programmer of the application by copying the file abstractLayouts.xml and by adding the required device-dependent data, the coordinates and the dimensions of the page items and icons, for example. Other device dependent information include the mapping between the icon names used by the Interaction Manager and the icons available on the access device (access device icon library).

After creating the general layout of the user interface, the client waits for the command that transports the single elements of the layout just loaded. Then, it continues listen the connection for detecting incoming updates. The client application must provide the management of the menu navigation and of the display of the appropriate tool tip messages when an interactive item is focused. Navigation can occur by using navigation keys (for example arrows keys or using rapid selection keys. The navigation order (tab order) of the interactive items displayed by clients is provided by the Interaction Manager while loading the various items composing the page. The Interaction Manager also imposes the tool tip message to be displayed in the opportune area when the interface items are focused. When a selection occurs, the client sends to the server the information relative to the pressed key or to the selected item identifier. The resolution of the association between the key and the interactive item is performed by the Interaction Manager.

3   Testing Environment

In order to test the proposed system, which has been developed in Java mainly for portability issues, a number of different devices and interfaces have been used. They are briefly presented in the following paragraphs and explained in more details in subsequent sections, followed by the explanation of the actual experimental set-up. The most relevant element is the domotic house located near the authors' laboratory. It is equipped with a home automation system produced by BTicino, an Italian industry for house electrical equipment. The house is maintained by C.E.T.A.D. [9]: a centre dedicated to the promotion, the development and the diffusion of technologies and innovative services for rehabilitation and social integration of elderly and disabled people. Another device is the MServ open source program [10], running under Linux, capable of remotely choosing and playing music files.

Two applications for Access Devices have been realized. The first is a Java application designed for a personal computer. The second is an Xlet, developed in JAVA-TV [11], designed for a digital television Set Top Box (DVB-T, with MHP capabilities).

3.1   BTicino MyHome System

The MyHome system developed by BTicino [6] is a home automation system able to provide several functionalities as requested by the increasing needs of users for smart and intelligent houses. These functionalities cover several aspects such as comfort configurations, security issues, energy saving, remote communication and control. The MyHome system realizes a domotic network. Control, in the BTicino system, is gained through a "house sever", and can be either local through a LAN connection, as experimented in this paper, or remote through an Internet connection or a telephonic network. Through a proprietary protocol, the gateway permits to manage all the devices of the house, e.g. lights, doors, shutters, etc. This component permits to interface the BTicino domotic network to the House Manager by simply exploiting its features, instead of connecting each device to the House Manager. It should be noted that the House Manager must poll the gateway to check the status of the domotic devices (the status of these devices can change, caused by people present in the home). This is due to the fact that the BTicino system does not support events natively.

3.2   Music Server (MServ)

This open source Linux application is basically a music player that can be controlled remotely, therefore acting as a server. It exposes a TCP/IP connection to receive commands such as play, next song, stop, etc., and to provide its status. MServ is normally accessible through a simple telnet application, but also HTTP CGI and several GUI applications are available for a more easy interaction with the system. The House Manager driver for MServ is therefore rather simple in this case. In fact, it only needs to exchange simple strings through a TCP/IP

```
<LAYOUTS>
    <LAYOUT>
        <LAYOUT_ID>1</LAYOUT_ID>
        <INF_ITEM>
            <INF_ITEM_ID>TITLE</INF_ITEM_ID>
            <XCOORD>325</XCOORD>
            <YCOORD>0</YCOORD>
            <XWEIGHT>340</XWEIGHT>
            <YWEIGHT>35</YWEIGHT>
            <COLOUR>BLACK</COLOUR>
            <BACKCOLOUR>ORANGE</BACKCOLOUR>
        <INF_ITEM>
        ...
        <INF_ITEM>
            <ITEM_ID>1</ITEM_ID>
            <XCOORD>365</XCOORD>
            <YCOORD>50</YCOORD>
            <XWEIGHT>260</XWEIGHT>
            <YWEIGHT>35</YWEIGHT>
            <COLOUR>BLACK</COLOUR>
            <BACKCOLOUR>LIGHT_GRAY</BACKCOLOUR>
        </INF_ITEM>
        ...
        <ICON>
            <ICON_ID>1</ICON_ID>
            <XCOORD>630</XCOORD>
            <YCOORD>50</YCOORD>
            <XWEIGHT>35</XWEIGHT>
            <YWEIGHT>35</YWEIGHT>
        </ICON>
        ...
    </LAYOUT>
    ...
    <ICONS_LIBRARY>
        <ICON name="LIGHTON" path="icons/light_ON.gif"/>
        ...
    </ICONS_LIBRARY>
</LAYOUTS>
```

Fig. 7. An excerpt of the layouts.xml file.

connection and to parse them appropriately (some informative message may be related to the status change caused by other connected clients, etc.).

3.3   Access Devices applications

Once built the House Manager configuration file (house.xml), which depends on the devices present in the home, the Interaction Manager configuration file (menu.xml) and the abstractLayout.xml file has been defined. The resulting menu structure is organized in different rooms: a main menu shows the rooms available in the home; for each room the devices to be controlled are presented as well as the menu items required for loading of more specific menus. These menus are used for managing scenarios or for more articulated devices, like shutters or the music server. However, for usability, the interface only allows three menu levels. Interactive items representing the menu items are associated to rapid selection keys (the numeric keys of the TV remote control). Intrusion alarms are settable The same abstractLayout.xml file, has been used to configure two clients: a Java application running on a laptop and an Xlet running on a STB emulator this last has been developed in JAVA-TV [11] and provides an area for displaying the TV program, reduced in size, during the house management.

3.4   Experimental Setup

The House Manager has been installed on a common PC with an AMD 1800+ processor, 512MByte of RAM and running a Java Virtual Machine (JVM). Two other similar PCs have been used for the Interaction Manager, the MServ while the PC-based user application used a entry-level laptop. All the three applications are expected to work fine on fairly less performing PCs. A simple Ethernet switch served as physical connection for the four computers and the BTicino gateway. The user application designed for a digital television STB Access Device, has been tested on an Open Source Emulator named XleTView [12]. The emulator and the developed Xlet have been installed to a personal computer similar to the others. Figure 8 shows the layout of the testing environment.

4   Results

A considerable number of tests have been performed, especially using the Xlet (Figure 9) designed for the STB access device. The access-device-dependent information needed in the access device configuration file proved to be very few in both of the experimented applications. The computational capacity required to the access devices results manageable and the communication between the Access Device and the Interaction Manager result not too intense (more precise figures are being gathered and will be evaluated in a near future). The House Manager addresses and manages well the different devices presents in the ambient. The latency between the command of the user and it's execution results acceptable.

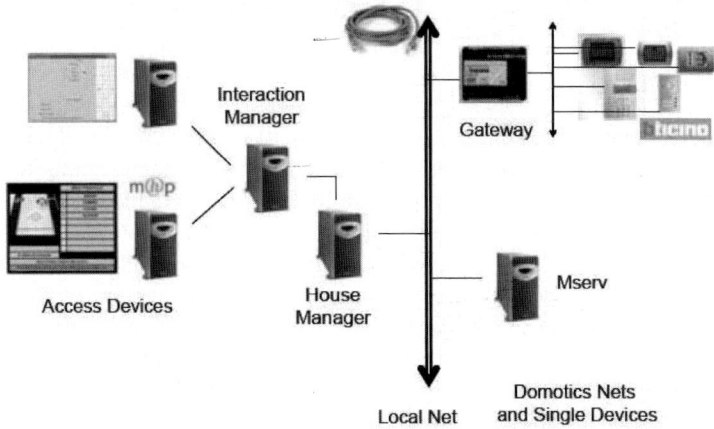

Fig. 8. The testing environment layout.

5   Conclusions

In the context of the Ambient Intelligence, this paper presented an architecture aimed at allowing users to control Ambient Intelligence in a domestic environment through a plurality of devices, including those with reduced capacity of elaboration and communication. The whole architecture has been illustrated and a prototype has been realized. A user interface application, designed for a digital television Set Top Box (DVB-T, with MHP capabilities), has been developed and used to test the architecture. Currently the authors are involved into two activities, related to this architecture. The first one is to redesign the architecture for permitting automatic device discovery, by means of an OSGi [13] compliant implementation of the House Manager. The Interaction Manager will be implemented, in this scenario, as an OSGi bundle.

References

1. Rick Harwig and Emile Aarts. Ambient intelligence: Invisible electronics emerging. In *Proceeding of the 2002 International Interconnect Technology Conference*, pages 3–5, San Francisco, California, 2002.
2. Dvb, digital video broadcasting. http://www.dvb.org.
3. Mhp. http://www.mhp.org.
4. Abascal J. Human-computer interaction in assistive technology: From "patchwork" to "universal design". In *Proceeding of the 2002 IEEE International Conference on Systems, Man and Cybernetics*, Hammamet, Tunisia, 2002.
5. Centro ricerche e innovazione tecnologica rai. http://www.crit.rai.it/eng/.

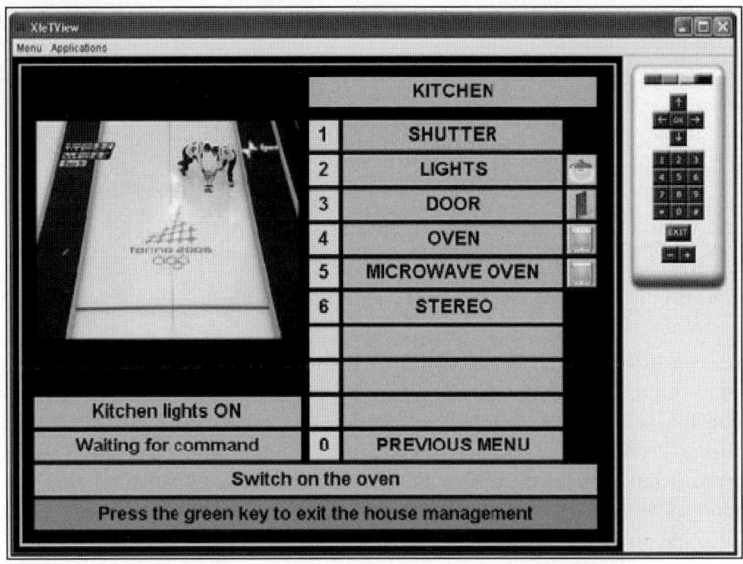

Fig. 9. The developed MHP Xlet running on XletView.

6. The BTicino MyHome system. http://www.myhome-bticino.it.
7. F. Corno P. Pellegrino, D. Bonino. Domotic house gateway. In *Proceedings of SAC 2006, ACM Symposium on Applied Computing*, Dijon, France, April 23-27 2006.
8. Zimeo E. Canfora G., Di Santo G. Developing java-awt thin-client applications for limited devices. *IEEE Internet Computing*, pages 55–63, Sept.-Oct. 2005.
9. C.e.t.a.d. (italian web site). http://www.cetad.org.
10. MServ a free, open source jukebox. http://www.mserv.org.
11. Java tv. http://java.sun.com/products/javatv/.
12. Xlettview. http://xletview.sourceforge.net.
13. OSGi alliance. http://www.osgi.org/.

Software Engineering Techniques Applied to AmI: Security Patterns

Francisco Sánchez-Cid, Antonio Muñoz, Daniel Serrano, and M.C. Gago

University of Malaga. Spain.
{cid,amunoz,serrano,mcgago}@lcc.uma.es

Abstract. The realization of the Ambient Intelligence concept entails many important challenges, but the most important barriers to this realization is the lack of adequate support for security. In this paper we present a conceptual model of our solution for building secure systems for AmI environments, taking as basis the concept of Security and Dependability (S&D) Pattern as a precise representation of validated S&D solutions and mechanisms. The main elements embedded in our solution framework (S&D library, monitoring interface and S&D Manager) are presented both conceptually, and also using a simple example scenario based on an hospital AmI environment.

1 Introduction

The EC Information Society Technologies Advisory Group (ISTAG), defines its vision of Ambient Intelligence as people surrounded by ubiquitous computers with intelligent and intuitive interfaces embedded in everyday objects around them, making the physical environments adapt and respond to users' needs in an invisible way in order to provide anytime/anywhere access to information and services.

As the current computing scenarios evolve to ubiquitous and dependable systems, new connection and interoperability challenges appear into scene and arises unforeseen security issues. While a good system design is necessary to enforce user requirements, this is not enough when system requirements change daily as users and devices appear and disappear at run-time.

The main aim of this paper is to present SERENITY approach to provide a framework for applying Security Engineering techniques to develop secure systems using the expertise of security engineers.

Several approaches have been introduced in order to capture the specialized expertise of security engineers and make it available for automated processing providing the basis for automated synthesis and analysis of the security and dependability solutions of software-based systems. Our proposal is based on the enhanced concept of *security patterns*, widely accepted as a suitable approach to represent and reuse the precise knowledge of security experts.

Present security patterns (most of them security *design* patterns) contain information about the problem, the requirements and the consequences of applying it, and the possible interactions with other well-known patterns. Nevertheless, as they do not present a pre-defined structure, and most of the times are written in a non-technique language, they are not suitable for automatic processing. This makes them appropriate when designing a system (usually with a modelling language like UML) but useless when the condition is to analyse and apply them while the target system is running. SERENITY framework aims to provide a Security & Dependability patterns library, structured not only for its automated processing but also for the monitor of the completeness and correctness of the applied patterns at run-time.

2   Related work

The existing approaches for modelling security and dependability aspects in Ambient Intelligence (AmI) ecosystems go from the Components through the Frameworks and Agents to the enhanced concept of Pattern.

Components capture expertise in the form of reusable software elements that solve a certain problem in a certain context, having a set of well-defined interfaces and an associated description of their behaviour [1, 2, 3]. The main interest of component composition is to build new systems from their requirements by systematically composing reusable components. In general, this concept is not appropriate to represent S&D solutions because security mechanisms can not always be represented as units that can be connected to the rest of the system by means of well defined interfaces.

Middleware-based approaches capture expertise in the form of standard interfaces & components that provide applications with a simpler façade to access a set of specialized, powerful and complex capabilities. An important problem with middleware-based approaches is that the computational cost of the middleware components is far too high for computing devices with limited capabilities. Finally, the security infrastructure of middleware systems is usually restricted to authorization and access control issues [4, 5]

Application *Frameworks* [6, 7] have emerged as a powerful technology for developing and reusing middleware and application software. Because frameworks are application templates, they are not well suited to cope with scenarios with high degrees of heterogeneity, dynamism and unpredictability. Likewise, this approach does not support secure interoperation with external (and not trusted) elements.

The *Agent* paradigm is especially well-suited for highly distributed environments such as AmI scenarios thanks to properties like: autonomy, interaction, context-awareness and goal-oriented nature. In the case of modelling security aspects, agent paradigms are much more limited [8], since an agent is an independent entity by definition and many security solutions can not be represented as agents.

Regarding with *Aspects*, the main idea is to simplify the development of a complex system by "isolating" the different aspects that must be considered in its development (functionality, performance, reliability, security, etc.). Unfortunately, aspects are mainly an implementation technique and not suitable to provide and manage S&D solutions as a whole [9, 10].

The concept of security pattern was introduced to support the system engineer in selecting appropriate security or dependability solutions. However, most security patterns are expressed in textual form, as informal indications on how to solve some (usually organizational) security problem [11, 12, 13, 14]. Some of them do use more precise representations based on UML diagrams, but these patterns do not include sufficient semantic descriptions in order to automate their processing and to extend their use [15].

Perhaps the first and the most valuable contribution as pioneer in security patterns as we know them at present, is the work from Joseph Yoder and Jeffrey Barcalow proposing to adapt the object-oriented solutions to recurring problems of information security [14]. In their own words, seven patterns were presented to be used when dealing with application security. A natural evolution of [14] is the work presented by Romanosky in [16]. It takes into consideration new questions that arise when securing a networked application.

Going one step down in the abstraction scale, Eduardo B. Fernandez in his work about authorization patterns [15] combines for the first time the idea of multiple architectural levels with the use of design patterns. In [17] they propose the decomposition of the system into hierarchical levels of abstraction.

The same author et al. offers in [18] a good source to study the historical approaches that have been appearing in the scientific literature as pattern systems for security. Wassermann and Cheng present in [19] a revision of most of the patterns from [14] and [17] and categorise them in terms of their abstraction level. In order to facilitate the reuse of security knowledge, variations of the design pattern template given in [20] are included in order to better suit the presentation of security specific information. In the field of web application protection, [21] is the source of some patterns for *Application Firewall* and *XML Firewall*.

The special needs of secure-ware systems and the constantly changing context in which the systems are designed nowadays arise some new problems that have an starting solution in works like the one presented by Cheng et al in [13]. The proposal consist of a template for security patterns that takes into account essential information that has not been necessary in the general design patterns but appears as mandatory in the new security context. Taking *Gamma et al.* [20] security patterns as source, a new patterns library is created by the addition of new relevant information (e.g. *Behaviour* or *Supported Principles* are two new field to describe the security pattern) and altering some existing fields (e.g. *Consecuences* is altered to convey a new set of possible consequences including confidentiality, usability, integrity, etc.).

Some security patterns have also been proposed for multiagent and Web Services systems. From the very beginning, the tendency has been to use the object oriented paradigm: in [22] an object oriented access control (OOAC) was firstly introduced as a result of consequently applying the object oriented paradigm for providing access controls in object and interoperable databases. Fernandez proposes in [23] some specific solutions oriented to web services: a pattern to provide authentication and authorization using Role-based access control (the so-called *Security Assertion Coordination* pattern) and a pattern for *XML Firewalls*. The *Security Assertion Coordination* pattern takes as source the abstract security architecture defined by SAML (the main standard to provide security for Web Services). However, a minor work has been done in the field of agent-based systems. A good start point is [24].

Some other authors have proposed ways to provide formal characterizations of patterns. The idea of precisely specifying a given class using *class invariants* and *pre-* and *post-conditions* for characterizing the behaviours of individual methods of the class is well known and is the basis of the *design by contract (DbC)* [25]. Evolutions of that approach have appeared and [26, 27] are some examples of that. Eden *et al.* [26] proposes to use logic formalism with an associated graphical notation to specify rich structural properties. However, it provides only limited support for specifying behavioural properties. In this sense, [27] has as main goal to preserve the *design integrity* of a system during its maintenance and evolution phases. Also Mikkonen in [28] focus his approach on behavioural properties. Here, data classes model role objects, and guarded actions (in an action system) model the methods of the roles.

3 Serenity Framework

3.1 Overview

Components, frameworks, middleware, and patterns have been proposed as means to simplify the design of complex systems and to capture the specialized expertise of security engineers and to make it available for non-expert developers. However, all these approaches have important drawbacks and limitations that hamper their practical use. Our approach aims at integrating the best of these approaches in order to overcome the problems that have prevented them to succeed individually. The main pillar to build solutions is the enhanced concept *of security pattern can capture security* expertise in a way that is more appropriate than other related concepts. Furthermore, because secure interoperability is an essential requisite for the widespread adoption of our model, trust mechanisms will be provided for patterns.

Therefore the objective of proposal is to work on the development and implementation of a tool-supported *integral framework for security and dependability* of software applications in AmI environments. Based on an integral model of security, our approach will consider not only static issues (related to secure systems development) but also dynamic aspects (related to monitoring and controlling the software at runtime). Validation mechanisms to deal with the dependences and the suitability of the applied solutions are used as well.

Due to the inherent dynamic nature of AmI environments, a flexible and runtime adaptable solution is required to confront the scenario. An appropriate solution should be succinctly described by means of an architecture composed of four elements: (i) a library of *S&D Security Patterns* available to bridge the gap between the new requirements and the security needs; (ii) a *monitoring interface* to control the execution of the security mechanisms; (iii) a *negotiation interface* to establish an appropriate framework configuration in case of: a change of the running context or an interaction with a new framework; (iv) and a *context retrieval interface* and an *end user interface* to detect new (and ever-changing) system requirements at runtime. Apart from that, in order to complete the architecture, a final element is necessary as well: a *security and dependability manager*, to coordinate the work of all the previous elements in order to look for one unique objective: apply sound security solutions to changing AmI environments.

S&D Patterns The *S&D patterns* contain descriptions of reusable and validated S&D solutions that include a precise specification, along with applicability conditions. Ideally, it should also include trust mechanisms. SERENITY's S&D patterns are precise specifications of validated security mechanisms materialised as files containing models that could be described using formal or non-formal languages (e.g. XML and logic-based language) to capture the expertise of security engineers with the objective of being used by automated means. S&D patterns include a precise behavioural description, references to the S&D properties provided, constraints on the context required for deployment, information describing how to adapt and monitor the mechanism, and trust mechanisms.

S&D patterns, along with the formal characterisation of their behaviour and semantics, are the basic building blocks of used by SERENITY's *integration schemes*. These schemes are used to specify ways for systematically combining S&D patterns into systems composed of dynamically collaborating elements that operate in mobile, heterogeneous, and highly dynamic ICT infrastructures. In addition, integration schemes are an invaluable guide when two different elements/devices try to collaborate in an AmI context: each one of the elements will include an instance of the SERENITY framework, and therefore, a negotiation phase between these frameworks starts when trying to interact reciprocally. The integration schemes serves as a consult instance for the SERENITY framework in order to establish the way in which the elements should be connected, the security & dependability implications of the negotiation, and the possible security risks emerging with the process.

The description of an S&D Pattern with the objective of being used by automated means in dynamic environments requires different aspects to be described. Some of these elements are:

- **Creator:** Identity of the creator/provider of the pattern.
- **Trust mechanisms:** Digital signatures and other mechanisms to guarantee that the pattern description corresponds to the pattern/solution, that it has been produced by the creator, and that it has not been modified.
- **Provided Properties:** Reference to the properties provided by the pattern. Properties have a timestamp and refer to descriptions provided by the entity that defines the property.

- **Components:** Every pattern will have several components that are used together in order to provide the pattern properties. Usually, they are the physical elements used by a pattern (e.g. a CCTV camera or a sensor, for a movement detection pattern).
- **Parameters:** One important aspect about components is that sometimes they can be generic. In this case, the component will appear as a *formal parameter* in the pattern. We define the terms *formal parameter* and *actual parameter* analogously to the typical definitions used in programming languages: The formal parameters are the names that are declared in the parameter list of the pattern. The actual parameters are the elements used when the pattern is instantiated (we could consider the pattern instantiation as a call to a subprogram).
- **Pre-Conditions:** A pattern is not necessarily a universal solution. This means that for the pattern to be successfully used to provide the declared properties, some pre-conditions must be met.
- **Static Tests Performed:** Security engineers will be responsible for the static testing of the pattern. This section will describe all relevant information regarding the static tests performed. We foresee that it might be necessary to develop mechanisms for the description of the tests, in a similar way as the description of the properties. This section will be useful for the monitoring mechanism, as some monitoring rules can be derived from it.
- **System Configuration:** In addition to the instantiation and integration of the pattern in the system it will be sometimes necessary to perform some actions before the pattern can be used in the system. Likewise, when the pattern is to be removed, some actions may also be necessary. In summary, the system configuration section of the description will describe the initialization and closing up processes, along with any other relevant system-specific information.
- **Monitoring:** This section describes all information necessary for the monitoring of the pattern. In particular, it must include which monitor to use, and the configuration of such monitor (events to monitor, rules, reactions, etc.)

Negotiation and Monitoring Interface Every instance of SERENITY framework as system will provide interfaces in order to allow interaction with other systems or other SERENITY instances; the following model presents this fact (figure 1). In summary, the framework will provide two main interfaces: On the one hand, it will provide a *negotiation interface* that will be used in order to establish the configuration of the interacting frameworks in a way that suits the requirements from all participants.

On the other hand, SERENITY frameworks will offer a *monitoring interface*. External elements interacting with an instance of the framework will be able to monitor that the behaviour of the framework is correct. The key to success is to capture security expertise in such a way that it can be supported by automated means. With this interface, we provide support for the dynamic supervision and adaptation of the security of systems to the transformations in ever-changing ecosystems.

Of course, the SERENITY framework will also feature the counterparts of these offered interfaces (required interfaces). It is foreseen that some external elements other than SERENITY frameworks will be able to interact with them by way of these interfaces.

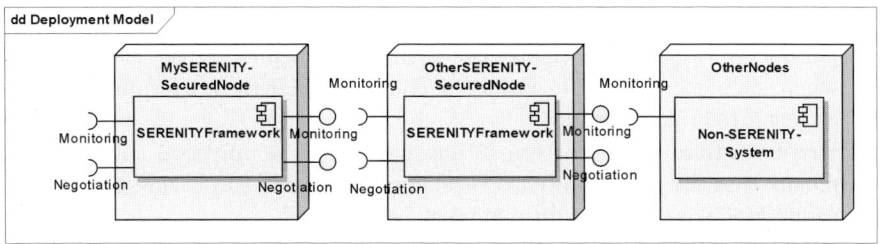

Fig. 1. Deployment model, more than one framework instance.

Context Retrieval Interface & User Interface Figure 2 presents an overview of the SERENITY framework. In the figure, the main interaction involves the *Security Experts* providing sound solutions and keeping track of the evolution of these solutions; the *Context Retrieval Interface* which captures critical information considered to be relevant as a change of the context can sometime alter the applicability of the current solutions; and the *end-user* (in some cases also with the system administrator role) who defines the preferences and the S&D requirements that the system have to meet.

The SERENITY framework is instantiated every time it has to be applied to a concrete scenario. The *end users* specify the security and dependability requirements for the systems they are designing by means of the *User Interface*. For that process, they use some specification tool (e.g. a UML modelling tool, the user menu from a PDA graphic interface, etc) fully integrated with the framework. The system then gets the information of the current context (using the *context retrieval interface*), looks for the most suitable solution fulfilling each one of the requirements, and starts the negotiation with the framework to choose the most appropriate pattern/s or combination of them to apply in the problem. Then, the end user does the final selection of a solution and the framework checks the dependencies and verifies the correctness of the selected model. After that, the run-time monitoring mechanism starts monitoring the workflow of the system. This will allow to react on time after any vulnerability on the requirements or to apply an improved solution (e.g. a new security patch), always taking into account that the patterns are in constant evolution and the system may decide that a new pattern has substitute the current one. More than that, the monitoring process appears as indispensable in case of change of

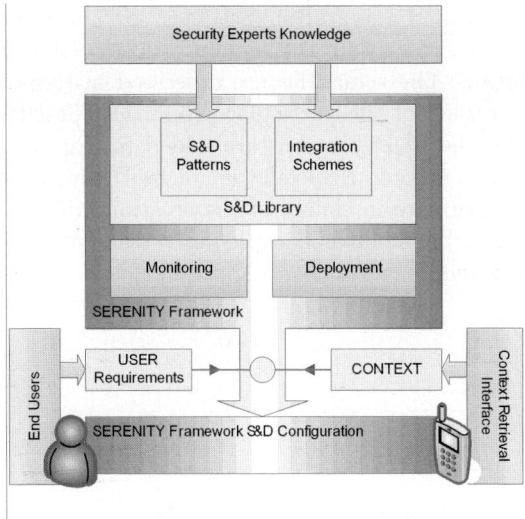

Fig. 2. Global SERENITY framework

the context of the system (e.g. a connection to a trusted network using your PDA, and then changing to an untrusted environment such as internet), when SERENITY has to adapt on-time the current solution in order to face the new situation.

Logical Components of the Architecture In order to describe this architecture, we need to combine different descriptions representing different aspects or elements of the ecosystem. In particular, we envision the following descriptions:

- **Description of Patterns.** For the moment we assume that this is common for S&D Patterns and Integration Schemes. The description of patterns includes two model elements: the *PatternCertificate* and the *S&DSolution-Semantics*.
- **Description of Properties.** Related to the description of the patterns is the description of the properties provided by them. This description must fulfil two basic objectives: (i) univocally identifying the properties, and (ii) enabling interoperation of the different properties. It corresponds to the *S&DPropertySemantics* in the conceptual model
- **Description of the User S&D Configuration.** This description contains the end-user S&D requirements (properties that must be enforced) as well as preferences and user amendments to pattern definitions. It corresponds to the *S&DConfiguration* in the model.

The logical model presented in figure 3 shows the conceptual elements that are used in SERENITY as well as its relations. On the right hand side of the model, S&D Patterns and Integration Schemes (*S&DPatterns*) refer to solutions (*S&DSolutions*) and contain the semantics (*S&DSolutionSemantics*) that describe such solution. The semantics are described in terms of the semantics (*S&DPropertySemantics*) of the particular properties (*S&DProperty*) provided by the solution. All the S&D patterns are added to a library, and the framework can use them to enforce a specific set of S&D properties defined by the user. Security Engineers are in charge of the creation and maintenance of such library. Solutions can be monitored by using certain monitoring mechanisms (*MonitoringMechanisms*).

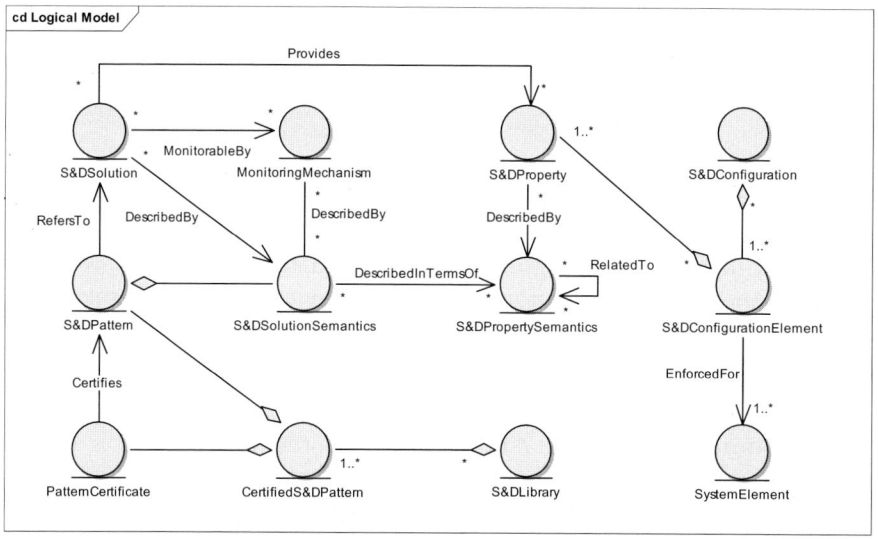

Fig. 3. Logical model, conceptual elements.

S&D Patterns and Integrations Schemes are certified by a special type of digital certificate (*PatternCertificate*). Therefore, the libraries of patterns (*S&DLibrary*) are composed of S&D Patterns and Integration Schemes that have a certificate, denominated certified patterns (*CertifiedS&DPattern*).

Finally, users will define the security and dependability requirements (*S&DConfiguration*) for their systems, which will contain a set of specific requirements (*S&DConfigurationElement*). Each specific requirement will specify a set of properties (*S&DProperty*) that must be enforced for a particular element of the system (*SystemElement*). With all this elements, the user benefits from a SERENITY framework instance that satisfies all the security requirements..

4   Instantiation and Adaptation of the Framework

The SERENITY framework is instantiated every time it is applied to a concrete scenario and device. Moreover, in AmI environments *S&D requirements* as well as external *context elements* should change so that some of the applied patterns are no longer applicable. It arises the necessity of defining a run-time protocol to respond to the new applicability conditions.

Figure 4 outlines the basic steps taken during a typical change of context situation. Once the framework is applied and configured, the *S&D Manager* component asks the *Monitoring Internal Interface* to start the monitoring process. Once an external condition changes (e.g. the user takes his laptop out of the office and tries to check his emails from his favorite restaurant), the framework gets into action. As the external context changes, the current system requirements are also modified. In this concrete example, a device previously connected to a trusted private network, suddenly tries to connect to the office email server from a non-trusted network (e.g. the wireless network of the restaurant), triggering the need of having a stronger encryption mechanism.

The change of context fires an event that is captured by the *External Monitor*, which automatically sends this hot information to the *Monitoring Internal Interface*. The Serenity Framework uses the information given by the motoring mechanisms to check the validity of the current configuration. It access into the *Active Patterns* component and detects that the pattern called "Secure connection over trusted network" is not applicable under this new conditions, alerting the *S&D Manager*. The framework creates a new query containing a set of search criteria in order to search into S&D Library for a new S&D Pattern or Integration Scheme applicable under the new conditions.

Once a new pattern is found, the *S&D Manager* starts the verification of its applicability. It is not only necessary to verify the application restrictions and requirements but also to establish the integration procedure regarding with the rest of the patterns placed in the *Active Patterns* component.

The *Integration Schemes* are basic items in this process. They convey the information that allows instantiating the concrete solution specified in the pattern, and to include it among the rest of the solutions of the *Active Patterns*. The result is the same Serenity Framework instance, but with a new adapted configuration.

5   An Application Example

After the specification of the SERENITY framework as well as the instantiation and adaptation process, we introduce a real world scenario. This will illustrate concrete Security & Dependability problems and how the framework deals with them.

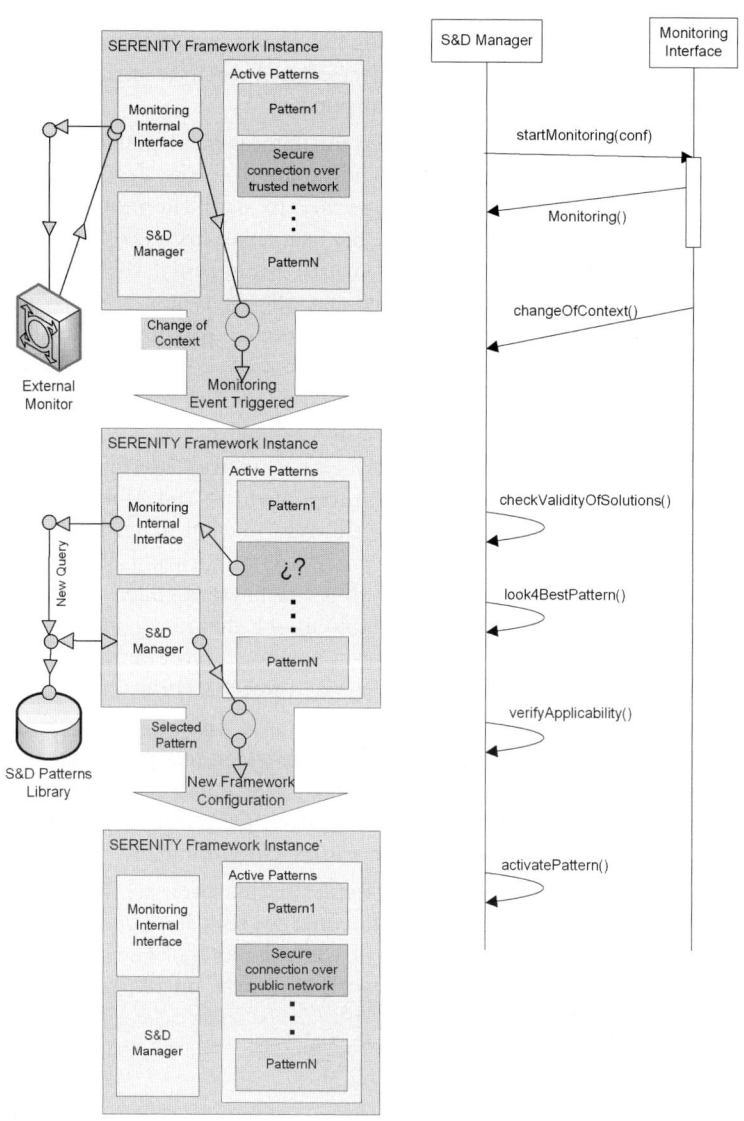

Fig. 4. Different phases on the adaptation of the Serenity Framework.

5.1   The Hospital scenario

In our hospital a doctor is in charge of several patients. The doctor visits each patient under his assignment and when necessary, he prescribes treatment based on his observations. In each visit, doctors retrieve patient health information that they take into account in order to prescribe treatments.

In addition, our hospital has two new technological advances that help both doctors and rest of staff members to improve their work.

The first one is the *patient tracking system*. Basically, this is a network of sensors that submits patient health data to a near computer. Patients' beds are provided with sensors able to monitor different aspects of their health (blood pressure, temperature, heart beats, breathing, etc.). All data collected by patient's sensors is managed by a room computer. Hospital Central Server (HCS) provide access to different rooms computers. Thus, each patient can be monitored using a computer connected to the hospital intranet.

The second advance offers the chance to check patient's health by the use of a mobile device, such as a PDA. By using this device the doctor is in permanent contact with his patients either if he is in the hospital or if he is outside the building. The mobile devices connect directly to the HCS using the secure intranet when doctors are inside the hospital boundaries, and try to use another method (Internet, GRPS, 3G ...) when the doctors change their location.

5.2   Analysis of the scenario

After a quick analysis, the previous scenario shows at least two key questions: (i) the patient's personal data is sent over the network and (ii) only the authorized doctors should be able to access to these data. Apart from that, taking into account the connection possibilities and the mobility of the system, we can distinguish two cases, graphically expressed in figure 5:

Case 1: The doctor requires information from *inside* the hospital. Using a mobile device such as a PDA, a smart phone or a laptop, the doctor is able to access the data of an assigned patient. Also, if a sensor detects critical levels in the measures, the patient tracking system can establish a direct connection with the doctor to alarm him. The hospital relies on desktop computers too. With a more flexible interface than a PDA, they could be used to perform more complex actions than a PDA or a smart phone. In this case, the doctor can not only access the data but modify or prescribe the treatment. The access control system has to take into account the type of device used to access the data, as well as the level of authorization of the doctor. More than that, it is important to assure that the person using the device is correctly authenticated against it, usually via a biometric system installed in the mobile device.

Case 2: The doctor requires the information from *outside* the hospital. In this case, the system has to allow the doctor to establish a secure connection with the internal system of the hospital through an insecure network. The system does not know a priori the origin of the user connection. The user can connect from a train station, using a public wireless network; from the train, using 3G

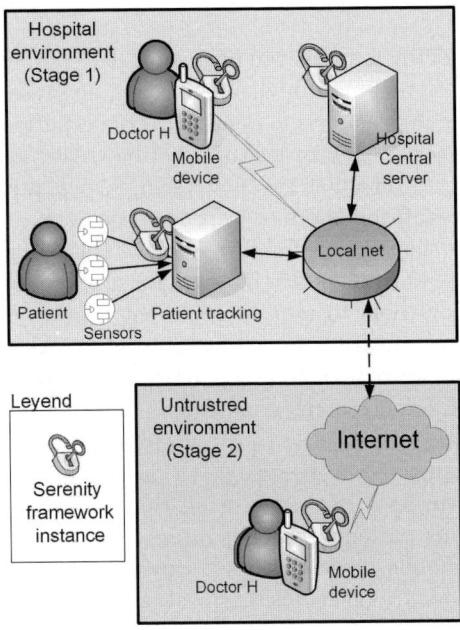

Fig. 5. Doctor-Patient connection Scenario.

via his mobile phone and so on. This situation arises two problems: the first is to achieve transparency for the connections, as the user has to be unaware of the connection changes; the second to provide security properties such as privacy, authenticity or authorization using an untrusted network. It is important to note that is much more difficult to maintain the privacy of the patient data once his information is going out of the scope of the hospital trusted environment. More than that, it is additionally difficult to make it transparent as the user is checking the patient data in his PDA while leaving the building from the reception of the hospital, in order to take a coffee in a place crossing the road. In a perfect AmI system, the device has to be able to switch between two operating modes without user notification, or with the slightest interaction from the user side.

5.3   Applying SERENITY to the scenario

The most suitable way to make all the previous system work is to provide every device with a mechanism to react on time to the constant and unpredicted changes of context. The SERENITY framework will be running in every device that composes the hospital system. Thus, there is one framework instance in each mobile device, (such as PDA, laptops or smart phones) and also in the computing elements permanently placed inside the hospital (such as the Hospital Central Server –HCS or the patient tracking system, composed by a set of sensors). It is important to highlight that every framework is fully operable by itself and, as seen in figure 3, they provide two interfaces to:

1. Negotiate with other boundary frameworks: after the PDA gets out of the scope of the internal network, it will negotiate with the HCS the most secure encryption algorithm according to HCS security requirements or preferences.
2. Monitor the critical elements of the framework: the change of connection from a trusted network to a 3G mobile connection fires a monitor trigger alerting about the no-longer validity of the current encryption algorithm.

Case 1 shows how a typical scenario should work once the requirements have been studied, the system modeled, and the application successfully installed. The system takes advantage of SERENITY once the number of end users starts growing without being predicted; once a new and smart device is now used by the surgeons to communicate with the patients and between each other; and generally speaking, once a new unpredicted requirement not present at the early stages of the system development, appears.

In case 2, the scenario introduces more complex features. The monitor interface present in the SERENITY framework that runs in the mobile device recognizes the untrusted environment (e.g. a 3G internet connection) and fires an event, alerting the system. As a result, the S&D manager collects all the information regarding with the new context of applicability and detects a violation in the protocol previously negotiated with the HSC framework. That protocol was valid only under the presumption of a local network, so the HSC will not allow the interchange of the patient data under the new circumstances. Quickly, the S&D Manager starts a negotiation with the HSC, and they establish that the connection will be possible if the mobile device is able to launch a VPN with the HSC. Again, the S&D Manager manages the situation and starts looking for a security pattern to achieve the new connection requirements. If a correct pattern is found, it is installed and placed with the rest of active patterns of the framework. The validity of the solution will be verified, and the monitoring mechanism for the new pattern will be activated.

Probably, as result of this adaptation the doctor will not be allowed to alter the treatment but he will still be able to check the patients' condition.

Finally, it is also necessary to remark the configurability of the framework. From the point of view of the patient, it should be desirable to achieve the desired grade of confidentiality. In case of being a public person, the threat for the medical data to be stolen is higher than the usual case. Therefore, it should be desirable for the user to establish which kind of data his doctor can freely share and which other data should be restricted. In any case, we are talking about a different configuration for a pattern common to every patient of the hospital. Consequently, users can adjust some SERENITY framework settings by using some parameters of the applied pattern.

6   Conclusions and Future Work

The work presented in this paper describes our approach to face the problem of security and dependability in AmI environments. The proposed framework, based on a solid conceptual design, embeds (i) the best solutions proposed by security experts by means of S&D patterns; (ii) a continuous interaction with the surrounding AmI environment; (iii) and the mechanisms to offer a meeting point between the requirements imposed by the environment and the solutions offered by the S&D library.

We also present an application example, where new heterogeneity and ubiquitous needs enforces the use of innovative security solutions. The monitoring mechanisms along with the instantiation and adaptation capabilities of the SERENITY framework allow to react at run-time and to adapt security solutions and configurations according to the new contexts in which the elements of the hospital (from doctors to PDA, through sensors) have to work as they are supposed to.

We are currently in the process of implementing these concepts in the ongoing SERENITY project. Our interest focuses on the realization of the concept of S&D Pattern, the semantic definition of security and dependability properties in order to guarantee the interoperability of S&D Patterns from different sources, and the provision of a trust infrastructure for the patterns.

References

1. Llewellyn-Jones, D., Merabti, M., Shi, Q., Askwith, B. (2004). "Utilising Component Composition for Secure ubiquitous Computing". Proceedings of 2nd UK-UbiNet Workshop.
2. Mantel, H., (2002). "On the composition of secure systems". Proc. of IEEE Symposium on Security and Privacy.
3. Shi, Q., Zhang, N., (1998). "An effective model for composition of secure systems," Journalof-Systems-and-Software, 43(3).233-44.
4. BEA White Paper. "BEA WebLogic Security Framework: Working with Your Security Eco-System". http://www.bea.com
5. Object Management Group. "The Common Object Request Broker: Architecture and Specification." http://www.omg.org
6. Llewellyn-Jones, D., Merabti, M., Shi, Q., and B. Askwith, "An Extensible Framework for Practical Secure Component Composition in a Ubiquitous Computing Environment". Proceedings of International Conference on Information Technology, Las Vegas, USA, April 2004.
7. Fayad, M., Johnson, R., Schmidt, D.C., (1999). "Building Application Frameworks: Object-Oriented Foundations of Framework Design". Wiley & Sons.
8. Boudaoud, K.; McCathieNevile, C. "An Intelligent Agent-based Model for Security Management," iscc, p. 877, Seventh International Symposium on Computers and Communications (ISCC'02), 2002.
9. Cigital Labs. "AOP: An Aspect-Oriented Security Assurance Solution" DARPA Project. http://www.cigital.com/labs/projects/1027/
10. Shah, V., Hill, F. (2003) "An Aspect-Oriented Security Framework". discex, p. 143, DARPA Information Survivability Conference and Exposition - Volume II.

11. Kienzle, D.M., Elder, M.C., "Final Technical Report: Security Patterns for Web Application Development." Available at
    http://www.scrypt.net/~ celer/securitypatterns/final%20report.pdf.
12. IBM's Security Strategy team. (2004). "Introduction to Business Security Patterns. An IBM White Paper". Available at
    http://www-3.ibm.com/security/patterns/intro.pdf.
13. Konrad, S., B.H.C. Cheng, Campbell, Laura. A., and Wassermann R., (2003). "Using Security Patterns to Model and Analyze Security Requirements". Proc. Requirements for High Assurance Systems Workshop (RHAS '03).
14. Yoder, J. and Barcalow, J. (2000). "Architectural Patterns for Enabling Application Security". Pattern Languages of Program Design. 4, 301-336. Reading, MA: Addison Wesley Publishing Company.
15. Fernandez, E.B., (2000). "Metadata and authorization patterns". Technical report, Florida Atlantic University
16. Romanosky, S., (2001). "Security Design Patterns", Part 1, 1.4.
17. Fernandez, E.B. and Pan, Rouyi, (2001). "A pattern language for security models". PLoP'01 Conference.
18. Torsten, P, Fernandez, E.B., Mehlau, J.I., Pernul, G. (2004). "A pattern system for access control". 18th IFIP WG 11.3 Conference on Data and Applications Security, (Sitges, Spain).
19. Wassermann, R. and Cheng, B.H.B., (2003). "Security patterns". Technical Report MSU-CSE-03-23, Computer Science and Engineering, Michigan State University, (East Lansing, Michigan).
20. Gamma, E., Helm, R., Johnson, R., and Vlissides, J. (1994). "Design patterns: Elements of Reusable Object-Oriented Software". Addison-Wesley, 1994
21. Delessy-Gassant, N., Fernandez. E.B., Rajput. S, and Larrondo-Petrie, M.M., (2004). "Patterns for Application Firewalls". PLoP'04.
22. Essmayr, W., Pernul, G., Tjoa, A.M., (1997). "Access controls by object oriented concepts". Proceedings of 11th IFIP WG 11.3 Working Conference on Database Security.
23. Fernandez, E. B., (2004). "Two patterns for web services security". Proc. International Symposium on Web Services and Applications (ISWS'04), (Las Vegas, NV).
24. Mouratidis, H., Giorgini, P., Schumacher, M., (2003). "Security Patterns for Agent Systems". In Proceedings of Eighth European Conference on Pattern Languages of Programs, (Irsee, Germany).
25. Hallstrom, J. O., Soundarajan, N., Tyler, B. (2004). "Monitoring Design Pattern Contracts". In Proc. of the FSE-12 Workshop on Specification and Verification of Component-Based Systems. pg. 87-94.
26. Allenby, K., and Kelly, T. (2001). "Deriving Requirements Using Scenarios". In Proc. Of the 5th IEEE International Symposium on Requirements Engineering. RE'01.
27. Hallstrom, J. O., Soundarajan, N. (2006). "Pattern-Based System Evolution: A Case-Study". In the Proc of the 18th International Conference on Software Engineering and Knowledge Engineering. San Francisco Bay, USA.
28. Mikkonen, T. (1998). "Formalizing design patterns". In Proc. Of 20th ICSE, pages 115-124. IEEE Computer Society Press.

A Serviceware Framework for Designing Ambient Services

Benjamin Hirsch, Thomas Konnerth, Axel Heler, and Sahin Albayrak

DAI-Labor
Technische Universitt Berlin
{benjamin.hirsch,thomas.konnerth,
axel.hessler,sahin.albayrak}@dai-labor.de

Abstract. This paper describes a serviceware framework for the creation of context-aware ambient services. Different communication standards can be found today, that are delivered through a multitude of devices. We propose to have them wrapped by a service execution engine which unifies access and service provision across different service domains. The framework provides basic building blocks for added security, multi-modal interaction, management, and comes with tools and a methodology.

1 Introduction

During the last few decades, computers went though a remarkable evolution. In the beginning, they were huge machines which needed experts to use and interact with them. As recently as 10 years ago, computers were found in many households but still needed some expertise to be used. Nowadays, computing ability is being embedded in all sorts of devices, more often than not invisible to the user. At the same time, the interconnectedness of those machines has risen accordingly. We have reached a point where it soon will be difficult to buy a product that does not have some sort of computing ability and interface to some host machine. As heterogenous as the devices are the possibilities of connecting them. Increasingly, this connection is based on ip-network and wireless technologies.

However, while devices are becoming smarter and get the ability to interface, they are still designed as single machines. Interaction between them is either impossible or very limited. Not only are different standards (such as UPnP [8], OSGi [3], webservices [21]) used, but devices generally have neither a notion of context nor the ability to interact autonomously, or with each other. As a result, users are being forced to interact with a growing number of devices and entities, many of which have overlapping functionalities [20].

For a number of years now the concept of ubiquitous computing has been a research area in its own right (e.g. [22]). However, while seamless connectivity is indeed an important aspect, we should not loose sight of the fact that it is not the solution to containing the complexity of our lives, and in fact adds to it.

What is needed are new ways of containing the chaos and complexity without losing the advantages that modern technology gives us [13].

The vision of ambient intelligence builds on the ubiquity of computing devices, but while the focus of ubiquitous computing lies in the embedding and constant availability of computation, ambient intelligence aims at making use of those entities in order to provide the user with an environment which offers services when and if needed by the user [2].

To this end, we propose a serviceware framework that allows to wrap the services being offered to us by new technologies, and create an environment which, while providing the all functionalities, does so in a human-centric way, combining and choosing between devices and services depending on the user, and the context of the user. Central to this is the concept of service, as opposed to device. In the remainder of this paper we will first go into a little more detail on the requirements for ambient intelligent services, and then proceed to describe out serviceware framework, which we believe is a (first step of a) solution to providing ambient intelligence to users today.

2   Requirements for Ambient Services

In order to develop ambient intelligent services, several preconditions need to be met. In the current state of affairs, home and office environments provide a host of devices, many of which have some IP interface. The range goes from mobile phones and PDA's to IP-enabled cooking devices and light switches to media centres to TV's and computers. We can classify these devices as multi-purpose and usually compute-able devices (like computers, phones, and PDA's), and "simple" devices who usually provide some sort of monitoring and control interface, but whose purpose is well defined.

Currently, a number of different protocols are employed, such as UPnP, OSGI, but also webservices and SOAP [11]. Common to them is that they have some notion of *service* that is provided to the network. However, while structures related to services are mostly implemented in those protocols, such as some form of service directory, or service call, it is instantiated in different ways. For example, an OSGi service essentially is some Java object with defined interfaces, while UPnP equates service with some device that provides it and the protocols to find and use it. Common to them however is that the service description

- is narrowly defined to cover only elements relevant to the task at hand,
- is semantically weak, i.e. has little or no semantic information, and
- is designed for machines.

In order to create an environment in which devices become less important and instead the services which they are providing

All those devices provide services to other devices, but also to the human users.

There are some aspects to ambient services that we will, in this paper, not focus on, but which are necessary to implement ambient services. The most important aspect is the one of user interface. As we have mentioned before, the goal of ambient services is to abstract away from device and towards context-aware service provisioning. Here, it is crucial that services can interact with the user using a number of different modalities, depending on the location, context, and availability of devices. For example, the address book service will present information with picture, eMail, and addresses when accessed by the user from a notebook computer, just the number and name when accessed from the user via a mobile phone with a small screen, and via a XML-message if accessed by another service as a step in a service-chain. Information about our approach to multi-modal service interaction can be found in e.g [17].

The availability of data is another aspect that needs to be addressed. In our scenario, as well as in the conception of the framework, we essentially assume that all services and devices are more or less constantly available. However, although this is a reasonable working assumption, provisions should be made for the case when connectivity fails. For example, it should be possible to use the address book in the home GAP-phone even if the server keeping the address book data is down for maintenance. This can of course be achieved by making use of a built-in address book service of the phone, but ensuring that the "main" address book service is always synchronised with the phone is not always straight forward.

Security and authentication issues are of extreme importance. If users cannot trust that the services they use in an ambient environment are private and secure, they will reject them, and ambience will never come to pass. On the other hand, secure and simple ways of communicating with and between services is a necessary element of ambient services. Authentication, single sign-on, public-key infrastructures, and encryption of content are all issues that need to be addressed, but would lead too far in the context of this paper. Let it be said that the framework we propose has components that address security and AAA (accounting, authentication, and authorisation).

3   The Serviceware Framework

Any framework for intelligent ambient services will have to provide solutions for many of the issues that derive from the domain. We will try to sketch the major challenges and propose a solution that addresses these issues.

3.1   Incorporating multiple domains

Taking a look at the current service landscape one quickly realises that today's services are powered by different technologies and server architectures like OSGi, JEE [16], .NET [5] and webservice technologies. Given the fact that providers and operators have already invested much into these systems and that existing software is unlikely to be adapted, we propose a solution that is able to incorporate those existing technologies. At the same time, our architecture will be open to future service technologies.

The general design of the framework is sketched in Figure 1. It consists of a service engine which interprets and executes our service description language, as well as a number of adapters that connect the engine to actual service providing entities and devices that are available in today's home and business environment. Each adaptor, as shown on the left of Figure 1, consists of domain specific invocation and control mechanisms, as well as a domain specific service directory which will be synched with the rich service directory of the service engine. The rich service directory, together with the engine, allows for example to expose UPnP-driven services to web-services. This way, a simple rule allows to output life weather data on a UPnP enabled television set. Note also that while we use JIAC IV [9] as a current implementation of the serviceware framework, we aim to extend the system, and view JIAC IV as one of the service providing entities. We give more detail on the current state of the implementation in Section 4.

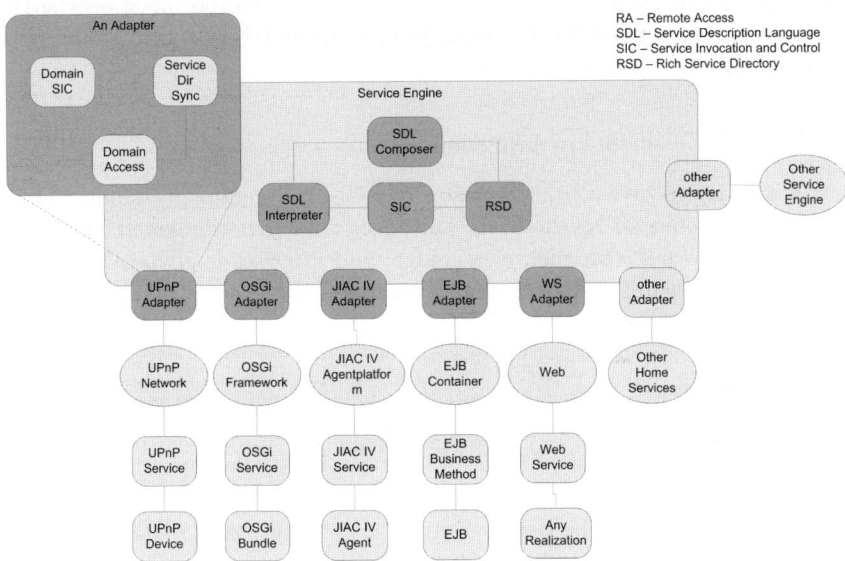

Fig. 1. The general design of the serviceware framework.

3.2   Heterogenous Networks and physical Distribution

From a users point of view, having to deal with different and incompatible access networks as well as physical distance is quite inconvenient. End users do not want to know about networking technologies, nor do they want to see them. Therefore a framework must not only be able to channel communication through different networks, it will also have to provide an abstraction of communication that enables the developer to implement the communication independent of network technologies. The adaption to the actual network, processes like address-translation and failure handling, and of course the selection of the optimal network in case of multiple networks being available, should be handled by the architecture, thus allowing the user as well as the developer to forget about network technologies.

3.3   Active Service Composition

Our central concept for the realisation of an intelligent and dynamic framework for ambient services is a Service Description Language (SDL) that describes not only the structure of a service but also its functionality in semantical terms. We are well aware, that there are already a number of (web-)service co-ordination and orchestration languages available on the market, such as BPEL4WS [6] or BPML [12] (to name but a few). However, we feel that these languages either merely aggregate function-calls without including the proper semantics that is needed for automatic service composition, or they focus too much on the theoretical aspects of service composition, thus being not very useful in actual development.

3.4   Service Description Language

We will now try to give a brief overview over the different aspects and elements that should be covered by the SDL. Following that, we will sketch the possible development-process with such a language, and afterwards give some examples of how the framework will modify and complete the designed system to adapt to the user-context.

Ontologies Ontologies are possibly the most important, and most difficult aspect — not so much because of their complexity, but because of the difficulty of describing the world. From the ideas of interoperability and openness follows the requirement that provider and consumer (to stay in the service domain) speak the same language, and interpret utterances the same way. While it may seem simple to create a common data structure used by both sides, the idea of openness requires this data structure to be publicly available and generally accepted. Therefore, current standardisation-efforts as well as the already available repositories of the ontology-community are well suited for our needs. Furthermore, if we want to apply some sort of semantical matching for service requests, ontologies are the best means to provide semantical information about the request, which can be used during the matching process.

Declarative Expressions In order to provide context-aware services, it must be possible to describe goals, or states-to-be, rather than actions, or things-to-do. Therefore, any service description language must include a (again semantically enhanced) pre- and post condition, i.e. the state changes that executing the service will bring about. BPEL3WS for example does not allow to describe desired states, and instead forces the user to describe a sequence of service calls. This way of describing components and states has two advantages that are vital to our approach. On the one hand, a developer may state what functionalities he needs to complete his service and the tools or a repository may find all services that can possibly help the developer at once. Compared to searching the repository simply for signatures (as it is common today), this semantical approach will return fewer and better matches.

Procedural Description In order to create complex control- and data-flows, a description language has to support the necessary constructs to express those. This includes things like sequential or parallel execution, as well as case differentiations and loops. This is common knowledge today — however, it is vital that any Service Description Language includes such constructs.

Composition of Services An important part of any service architecture is the composition of services. We think, that while the developer should design his application from start to end by combining and composing services, it is also important that the designed control-flow is loosely coupled. By using semantical descriptions for the parts of an application, rather than tightly linked calls, it will be possible to exchange and replace functionalities at runtime. This will be of advantage especially in open and dynamic environments, where the availability of services and providers may not be forseen.

3.5   Designing complex Services

Given the descriptions of the last section, we will try to sketch a scenario of how a SDL may be used in development of context aware services. Let us assume, our developer wants to create a service that looks up cooking recipes from the web, filters the available recipes according to the users preferences, and afterwards displays the recipes on a device that is close to the user.

So the list of required sub-services would look like this:

- Fetch_Recipes_Service
- Fetch_UserPreferences_Service
- Filter_Recipes_Service
- Find_nextScreenToUser_Service
- Present_Recipes_OnScreen_Service
- UserSelect_Recipe_Service
- Present_Recipes_ViaVoice_Service

Now let us assume that the *Fetch_UserPreferences_Service* already exists from a different Scenario and that there is a generic Service for localisation (*Find _nextScreenToUser_Service*), as well as services for handling of data (*Present_ Data_OnScreen_Service, UserSelect_Data_Service*).

The development process for creating a recipe service would look as follows:

First, the developer creates the core functionality of his application, i.e. he creates a Service that looks up the recipes, as well as filtering mechanisms for the retrieved recipes according to a user profile. He can do this without knowledge of the other services, as all data handled by the framework is represented by ontologies that are publicly available.

During the development of the filtering service, the developer realises that the profile-data needs to be retrieved in order to be available for filtering. Thus he queries the framework for existing services that return user profiles. The framework (in this case the development environment) responds with the *Fetch_UserPreferences_Service*, and the developer only has to include this service into his process model.

This first scenario describes a process that is omnipresent in software- development. The developer needs a functionality with a certain signature, looks it up and includes it into his application. While it is nothing special to look up services by their signature, we are trying to enhance this look-up process by introducing semantical descriptions of the services, and this improve lookup speed and results. To illustrate this, let us continue our example:

Once the developer is sure to have a selection of appropriate recipes, he needs to have the user select a recipe. Therefore the recipes need to be presented to the user. Accordingly, the developer looks for a service that is able to present recipes. Let us assume now that no such service exists yet — however, there is a generic service for the presentation of data on a screen. Even though the developer was looking for services that take recipes as input, the framework is able to recommend the *Present_Data_OnScreen_Service*, as recipe is a subcategory of *Data*, and the semantic matching engine is able to make this generalisation.

Furthermore, when the developer tries to use the Service *Present_Data_ OnScreen_Service*, he is informed, that this service needs a display-device as input. He looks up services that return screens in a house, others finds the *Find_nextScreenToUser_ Service*, which not only returns an available screen but also the one that is closest to the user.

To complete our service, the developer now only needs to include the service for selection of recipes (*UserSelect_Recipe_Service*) which is a user-interaction service, and thus available in the same way as the data-presentation service. To keep things simple, our developer decides to re-use the same display service for the final recipe that he already used for the list of available recipes. Thus the application is finished.

So far, our scenario describes, how it is possible to design complex applications in a rather simple and direct way. The developer can concentrate on the control- and data-flow, and does not have to worry about the internals or the data-types of individual services. However, we can expand this scenario even further.

Once the service is deployed, a user may start it, select a recipe and afterwards move from the living room to the kitchen, as this is the place where he would actually need the service. Now lets say that there is no display in the kitchen, but only a speaker system. As the developer stated, that the recipe should be displayed on the nearest screen to the user, this would normally lead to either displaying the recipe in the wrong room, or, if the display service explicitly states that the user should be in the same room as the screen, a failure of the service. However, given a semantical description of the action, i.e. that the data should be presented to the user, the runtime engine may now decide to use a different display method rather that letting the service fail. Now the *Present_Recipes_ViaVoice_Service* may be semantically equivalent to the *Present_Data_OnScreen_Service*, and thus be selected by the system. Thus the recipe is read to the user, rather than displayed on a screen and is still successful. [17] describes a multi-modal user-interface that would be able to achieve the scenario described.

3.6 Managing Services

From an operators point of view, maintenance of a system is something that definitely has to be addressed. While the deployment of a service on a running infrastructure is only the beginning, monitoring and control of active services also play an important role. This is especially important for intelligent and autonomous services, as these may show all kinds of unexpected behaviours that are hard to track down. Today, the management-concepts of networks and telecommunication-systems are quite advanced. We propose to use and adapt these techniques for high level services. A part of this infrastructure has also been implemented JIAC.

3.7 User Access to Services

An important aspect of services is their accessibility. As the name *ambient services* suggests, we will not only try to make services available to the user always and anywhere, but we will also try to make them adapt to the situation and the location of the user. To achieve this, it will be necessary to enable the framework to provide access to all kinds of devices. Furthermore, it has to be able to choose an appropriate user interface as well as a reasonable amount of information for that user interface. As an example, for a voice based email-service, it is certainly better to just report the subjects of the received emails, rather that read the whole email to the user. We refer to [17] for an example of multi-modal user interaction.

User data and profile-information are another aspect that should be considered by a framework. While in the modern world, users are already used to storing much of their data in computer systems, the accessibility of this data is still an issue. If you take a simple address book as an example, many people have different address books for their phone, for work and for their mobile phone. While it may be quite sensible to separate this data, synchronisation and accessibility is definitely an issue, e.g if you want to keep the entries of your telephone at home synchronised with the entries of your mobile phone. On the other hand, if you can manage to wrap these address books with services, that allow you to access the information, and at the same time find ways to make these services accessible anywhere, synchronisation is not much of an issue any

more. As this is likely to hold true for other data as well, our frame work will
have to provide means to access and propagate data from anywhere.

4   Current Status

The last few sections described work in progress. However, we do not start from
scratch, and base our ambient framework on research and work that has been
done already. Specifically, we use our agent-based serviceware framework JIAC
[9] as a starting point.

4.1   The JIAC Framework

JIAC IV [9] is a FIPA-compliant [7] agent framework *JIAC* (Java-based Intelligent Agent Componentware). In the following we will describe the characteristics
of this agent framework. The framework has been used to implement a number
of different projects, such as a personal information agent [1] and entertainment
solutions [23].

JIAC consists of a run-time environment, a methodology, tools that support
the creation of agents, as well as numerous extensions, such as web-service-
connectivity, device independent interaction [17], an owl-to-*Jadl* translator, a
OSGI-connector and more. An agent consists of a set of components, rules, plan
elements, and ontologies. Strong migration is supported.

JIAC's component model allows to exchange, add, and remove components
during run-time. The components interact among each other by agent internal
messages. Standard components (which themselves can be exchanged as well) include a fact-base component, execution-component, rule-component, and more
[19]. These components provide individual messages to manage the appropriate
actions, e.g. the *MonitorGoalMessage* executed by the *GoalBean* allows to sub-
scribe for changes on the goal stack. A *JIAC* agent is defined within a property
file which describes all elements that the agent consists of.

JIAC is the only agent-framework that has been awarded a common criteria
EAL3 certificate, an internationally accepted and renowned security certificate
[10].

Agents are programmed using the language *Jadl* [15]. It is based on three-
valued predicate logic [14], thereby providing an open world semantics, and implements an BDI [4] approach. It comprises four main elements: *plans elements,
rules, ontologies,* and *services.*

Communication is based on services. An agent, in order to achieve a goal, first
tries to find a plan element whose effect matches the goal. If this plan element has
pre-conditions, a planning component creates a plan which has to be executed in
order to achieve the goal. Plan elements can be atomic actions, complex actions
(written in *Jadl*, which in turn can trigger goals), and services. This means that
agent communication happens transparent to the planning component. A service
invocation consists of several steps, and is based on a meta-protocol, an extension
of the FIPA request protocol. First, the agent contacts the Directory Facilitator

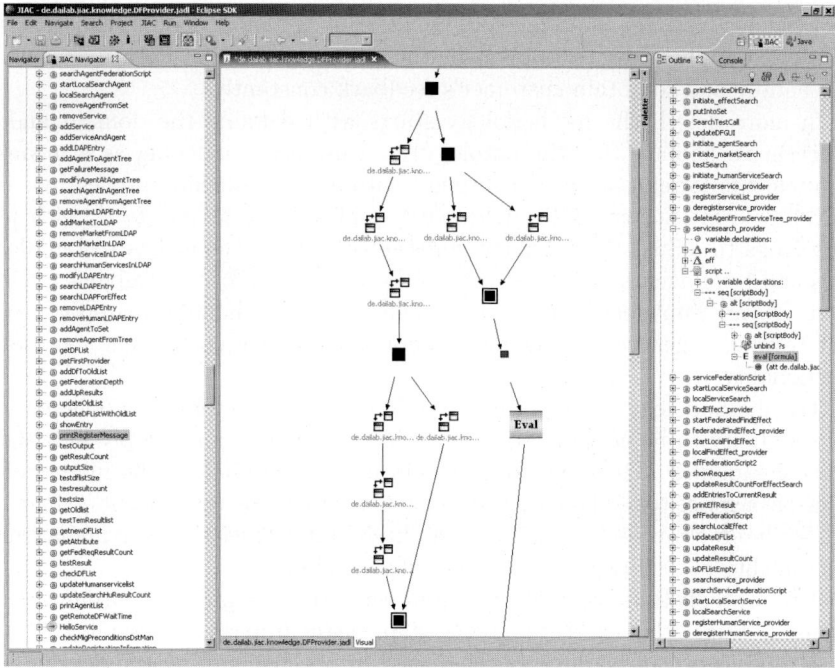

Fig. 2. Our Service Development Environment

(DF) in order to receive a list of possible services that could fulfil the current goal. After selecting a service and informing the DF, the agent receives a list of agents providing that service. Now an optional negotiation protocol can be executed with which the actual service provider is chosen. Only now the actual service protocol is executed. The meta protocol handles service-independent elements like security, accounting, communication failures, and other management-related issues.

4.2   Methodologies and Tools

JIAC provides a set of tools which simplify the creation of agents. This includes (Eclipse-based) textual and graphical tools for the design and creation of agents and their elements, such as ontologies, plan elements, services, and goals. Furthermore, there exist tools that support various extensions of *JIAC* like a security infrastructure.

Our methodology represents a process guiding the service developer from defining early requirements up to deploying an solution. We use the concept of agents which provide services to guide the developer. This way, large dynamic systems can be modularised and its complexity can be controlled.

Following this methodology, the service developer is encouraged to develop first those parts that are not captured by our domain library. He is supported by a life-cycle model, enabling him to identify urgent and important parts of his service application, to implement the whole application iteratively and incrementally and to obtain customer's feedback constantly.

In more detail, the methodology starts with defining the domain and interaction vocabulary (i.e. the ontology) and use case modelling as a means of requirements formalisation. It continues with a role modelling process where it allows to form encapsulated functionality and services as interfaces with feedback loops to adjust the ontology. Subsequently a developer has to bundle his roles and have agents instantiate the roles in order to form a ambient environment. During implementation and deployment the methodology supports agent unit testing, a generic debugging concept, and service component monitoring functionality.

The methodology is role-based. A role consists of several components with the capability to be adapted to a concrete environment and simply be plugged into a component. The main focus herein lies on reusability. The methodology relies on a repository allowing a developer to reuse his components, their reasoning, interaction and security capabilities, infrastructure, and management functionality as well as his domain specific capabilities.

A set of tools that are built into an integrated development environment (see Figure 2) guides the user through the steps defined by the methodology.

A repository can be directly referenced by the IDE during the development and deployment phase. A service developer can freely design the flow of control using existing service components. Data flow will be interfered from the ontological dependencies.

5   Conclusion and Outlook

In this paper, we have described a serviceware framework which we believe can be used as a basis for the creation of provision of ambient services. We have identified a number of requirements that need to be met by the framework. As today's devices use a number of different service concepts, the framework needs to not only be able to talk to the devices, it needs to have a service description language that encompasses the service concepts of the device-specific protocols. This way, the services provided by the devices can be used in arbitrary order and connection. Furthermore, some basic requirements such as security, need to be supported by the framework.

The described framework is currently under development — as we base our design and parts of the implementation on the JIAC IV framework that has been developed by us, we have already solutions for many of the issues that a serviceware framework for ambient services will need to address, such as multimodality, security, and more. The integration of current home and enterprise-technologies in order is one of our priorities now. As described in this paper, we develop a service description that encompasses different service domains and allows to address services (of any of the domains) in a semantical fashion. While we acknowledge that there are many unsolved issues, and elements that we do ignore that the moment, we believe that our system will be yet another step in the direction of providing ambient intelligence to the user.

References

1. S. Albayrak and M. Dragan. Generic intelligent personal information agent. In *International Conference on Advances in Internet, Processing, Systems, and Interdisciplinary Research*, 2004.
2. M. Alcañiz and B. Rey. New technologies for ambient intelligence. In Riva et al. [18], chapter 1, pages 3–15.
3. O. Alliance. Osgi service platform core specification, release 4, August 2005.
4. M. E. Bratman. *Intentions, Plans, and Practical Reason*. Havard University Press, Cambridge, MA, 1987.
5. M. Corporation. .net. http://www.microsoft.com/net/.
6. I. developerWorks. Business process execution language for web services. http://www-128.ibm.com/developerworks/library/specification/ws-bpel/.
7. FIPA. FIPA ACL Message Structure Specification. FIPA Specification SC00061G, Foundation for Intelligent Physical Agents, Dec. 2002.
8. U. Forum. Device security and security console standardized dcps. http://www.upnp.org/standardizeddcps/security.asp.
9. S. Fricke, K. Bsufka, J. Keiser, T. Schmidt, R. Sesseler, and S. Albayrak. Agent-based Telematic Services and Telecom Applications. *Communications of the ACM*, 44(4):43–48, Apr. 2001.
10. T. Geissler and O. Kroll-Peters. Applying Security Standards to Multiagent Systems. In M. Barley, F. Massacci, H. Mouratidis, and P. Scerri, editors, *First International Workshop on Safety and Security in Multiagent Systems*, pages 5–16, July 2004.
11. W. X. P. W. Group. Soap version 1.2. http://www.w3.org/TR/2003/REC-soap12-part0-20030624/, 2003.
12. B. P. M. Initiative. Business process modeling language specification. http://xml.coverpages.org/BPML-2002.pdf.
13. IST Advisory Group. Ambient intelligence: From vision to reality. In Riva et al. [18], pages 45–68.
14. S. C. Kleene. *Introduction to Metamathematics*. Wolters-Noordhoff Publishing and North-Holland Publishing Company, 1971. Written in 1953.
15. T. Konnerth, B. Hirsch, and S. Albayrak. Jadl - an agent description language for smart agents. *Proceedings of DALT06*, 2006.
16. S. D. Network. Java platform, enterprise edition. http://java.sun.com/javaee/index.jsp.
17. A. Rieger, R. Cissée, S. Feuerstack, J. Wohltorf, and S. Albayrak. An Agent-Based Architecture for Ubiquitous Multimodal User Interfaces. In *The 2005 International Conference on Active Media Technology*, 2005.
18. G. Riva, F. Vatalaro, F. Davide, and M. Alcaniz, editors. *Ambient Intelligence: The Evolution Of Technology, Communication And Cognition Towards The Future Of Human-Computer Interaction*. O C S L Press, March 2005.
19. R. Sesseler. *Eine modulare Architektur für dienstbasierte Interaktion zwischen Agenten*. Doctocal thesis, Technische Universität Berlin, 2002.
20. W. Weber and J.M. Rabaey and E. Aarts, editor. *Ambient Intelligence*. Springer Verlag, 2005.

21. W3C. Web services activities. http://www.w3.org/2002/ws/.
22. M. Weiser. Hot topics: Ubiquitous computing. *IEEE Computer*, 1993.
23. J. Wohltorf, R. Cissée, and A. Rieger. BerlinTainment: An agent-based context-aware entertainment planning system.
    IEEE Communications Magazine, 43(6):102–109, June 2005.

Context-Aware Adaptive Trust

Silke Holtmanns and Zheng Yan

Nokia Research Center, Itämerenkatu 11-13, 00180 Helsinki, Finland
{Silke.Holtmanns,Zheng.Z.Yan}@nokia.com

Abstract. Trust is a very complex and multi-disciplined concept. In this article we start by analysing social trust scenarios to derive abstract trust concepts. From these abstract trust concepts a context aware adaptive trust concept is developed. The context aware adaptive trust concept takes into account the dynamics of trust and the context based grouping of trust properties. The implementation of the concept will be subject to further evaluation and research.

1 Introduction

The description of the exact meaning of the term *trust* is a complex task. The usual approach is the "A trusts B about some thing, person or issue" raises in a normal everyday context the following immediate thoughts:

- Trust evolves and changes dynamically and can be very different in phases of a trust relationship.
- Trust has a quite varying degree (multilevel) and scope, depending on the context or other factors. Some factors are subjective and other ones are explicitly measurable.
- Trust is subjective and usually not strictly transitive, and can not be transferred from entity A to entity B.

Most technical trust management systems focus on protocols to establish a trust base for a particular context (e.g. password), generally based on some security requirements. Another approach is to utilize a trust policy language to allow the trustor to specify the criteria for a trustee to be considered trustworthy [7]. Most trust solutions do not acknowledge that trust changes over time dynamically and have no mechanism for monitoring the fine-grained change in a trust relationship.

In [10] trust is regarded as a plain level concept ("meso"), where people change from one trust level to the next. This concept reflects trust relationships that can be clearly grouped together, but dynamic changes and trust relationships that are difficult to group (e.g. process, that may request the same resources) are not covered fully by this approach.

A cross-disciplinary approach that, still missing the full dynamical aspects of trust, has been taken by Rousseau and others [16], which describes the notion of trust as "Trust is a psychological state compromising the intention to accept vulnerability based upon positive expectation of the intention or behaviour of another". The dynamical adaptation of the trust relationship between two entities requires a sophisticated trust management. In this article we investigate an adaptive trust management system concept, that satisfies the characteristics above and has the ability to alter a course of action when new information becomes available i.e. the ability to take corresponding measures to manage trust that may be influenced by a dynamically changing environment or context. The concept will be deducted by abstracting classical social trust scenarios into an adaptive trust management concept. This adaptive trust management concept needs then to be implemented and evaluated further. Since trust is a very human concept, a trust management concept needs to be evolved in an interactive manner, collecting and integrating as much feedback as possible. For this reason, the adaptive trust management concept is presented here, so that the scientific expert community feedback can be taken into account in the next steps of the research work.

2   Social Trust Scenarios

Social trust is a key component for the social capital to facilitate coordination and cooperation for mutual benefit [14]. In [8] social trust is regarded as the product of experience and the perceived trust is constantly modified and updated with our trustful and distrustful feelings in response to changing circumstances. As a result, levels of trust reported in social surveys are a good indicator of the trustworthiness of the environment and societies in which the survey has taken place. The trust scores give us a good insight about societies and social systems than about the personality and social types living in them. Trust in general is subjective property [3], and some aspects of trust are measurable [12] , but the factors that are the basis for personal trust people are generic:

– **Common ground**

We tend to trust people that have a common ground with us e.g. family, work colleagues, church community, people from same village, hobby club etc. These relationships build through common activities build the foundation of our personal trust network.

– **Common experience and type of experience**

A common experience or jointly mastered hardship gives us trust in a relationship. This can be a joint project or some other experience. Some companies that offer social binding courses for companies that just merged offer common climbing experiences to facilitate the feeling that "one can not without each other and we depend on each other".

– **Interaction frequency / relationship history**

Long standing relationships or people we deal constantly with receive a higher level of trust e.g. you can pass, I know who you are, old schoolmates. A bad experience might ruin a relationship that just has been set up, a long standing relationship is more likely to "clarify" the issue. Also, trust is quite sensitive, in the sense that one bad experience can change a trust relationship completely.

– **General connection (friend-of-a-friend)**

People that are tight in a close social network and have good relationship are usually regarded as trustworthy "via reputation" e.g. my neighbour also hired this plumber. The closer the link is, the higher the trustworthiness of the reputation is judged, but not only the closeness of the link is important, also the reputation of the "evaluator" is important.

– **Organizational and institutional factors**

A trusted third party might vouch for the trustworthiness e.g. a banking employee is trustworthy with your bank account, police officer can stop your car. This kind of trust usually is closely bound to one context setting.

– **Context dependence**

Trust is context dependent e.g. bound to a purpose or task. Seldom trust extends to all aspects of life, trust relationships often result on a per-need basis e.g. handing the key to the neighbour to water the flowers during absence.

3   Trust Abstraction

"Technology cannot solve social problems" (Joseph Weizenbaum in a speech at the FIFF Forum fuer Informatiker fuer Frieden und Gesellschaftliche Verantwortung Meeting in 1997 in Paderborn, Germany). Our world as grown very complex and many types of interactions happen automatically or semi-automatically. How can we ensure that the principles that influence our social trust relationships also apply to the "technical interactions"? In the previous section we analysed social trust, now we want to extract from these technical principles that help the users of the trusted system to manage their ever-more complex interaction patterns in a way they are used to.

– **Trust is time dynamic [7]**

The trust relationships are subject to natural decrease and usually get "the old level or better" if some interaction has happen. The longer the relationship period the slower is the decrease in trust. Hence, automatic trust adaptation should take place, but also the length of the whole trust relationship needs to be considered.

– **Trust changes are event oriented**

Trust is created or caused on event basis (or time basis, see previous bullet). Usually, an event related to another person changes the trust relationship. It does not necessarily mean, that the other person is directly involved. The trust relationships need to be modifiable on event basis.

– **Trust can be inherited to some degree [1]**

In mathematical terms trust is non-transitive relation i.e. A trusts B, B trusts C does not imply that A trusts C. But actually, this is not entirely accurate, since the relationship that A has with B will influence the trust relationship that A will have to C, at least for creating an initial trust. The typical social format of this is a recommendation by a good friend.

– **Trust is context based**

The trust relationship is most often context based e.g. work related, location related, hobby related, task or purpose related, etc. This implies that automated systems should only trust context-box-wise, like described by [2]. Trust is often limited time-wise and bound to a specific action, event or process. Context can often be structured hierarchically, if you trust someone to drive your car, then you would most likely also give him your car keys or the keys to the garage.

– **Trust can be caused / modified by non-detectable events**

However ubiquitous our environment might become, there will always be trust relationship changes due to non-machine detectable events, else we would be completely controlled and monitored and loose our humanity. Appearance, body language, facial gestures, knowing of habits etc are often triggers for these kinds of non-detectable events.

4   Context-Aware Adaptive Trust Concept

The "Why" in a trust relationship is the key to our adaptive trust concept. Context has been defined in various ways [13]. We still not restrict our context-aware adaptive trust concept to e.g. only location, but take the context definition of [5], who defines context as:

"any information that can be used to characterise the situation of entities".

We structure entities, which can be applications, other users or agents that act on behalf of users into a context-based trust graph. In our example, we use the wording access rights, in other words, an application has rights (use, read, write, etc) to specific context like system resources, data fields, bandwidth. The position in this graph indicates the context-based trust level and henceforth rights this entity has. The position in the graph changes, based upon events or during time. It is possible that two entities hold the same position in the trust graph, as shown in Figure 1. The position in the trust graph indicates the "trustworthiness" of that entity, for example application 1 is more trustworthy than application 2, 3, 4 and 5, since it has a set of access rights that are a subset of the access rights of application 2, 3, 4 and 5. But the trustworthiness of application 1 can not be compared to the trustworthiness of application 8, since there is no directed path between these two applications. This reflects the fact, that application 1 and application 8 have disjoint access rights and therefore their trustworthiness is not comparable.

Each node in the graph represents a resource requesting entity. If the context changes, due to some event or natural change (time dynamic trust change), then the trust graph will be adjusted accordingly. To each entity a set of rights and conditions is connected, these are usually bound to a resource or group of resource. In the figure below the nodes are a set of applications (sometimes also called agents) that wish to request access to resources e.g. personal data, processing power, memory capability, network capability, etc. For the access to the resource some rights are attached e.g. a health care application should be able to obtain processing power and network resources. The position in the context based trust graph represents the priority between the different applications that wish to act upon a resource. If the resource and the access right might have also some priority attached to it or a volume indication (e.g. for processing power or network bandwidth). Below we outline such a trust graph for simple access rights to different resources. The structure of the graph indicates some sort of inheritance, the applications on the upper layers inherit the trustworthines (i.e. rights) of the applications of the linked lower layers, but may have additional rights on their own.

If priorities are attached to the access rights, then each application has a dedicated priority with regard to each access right as indicted in the Figure below. The application developer or the one responsible for the application (e.g. in a mobile scenario this may be the manufacturer or operator) can issue the access rights to the applications. Based on security or performance considerations and on importance of the applications the access rights can be assigned e.g. a health application should be able to obtain any bandwidth it is needed for an emergency message. The arrow specified the access rights ownership of the applications, while the label of the arrow indicates the priority of access rights. P0 is default priority, and priority P2 is higher than priority P1.

An entity in the graph (here in the examples, applications and connected rights to resources) moves in this trust graph based on some events or natural change of rights due to change of trust due to "natural decrease". Now we outline, how the graph changes due to change of trust in an application. In this article we will not elaborate on how the actual change in trust is determined and calculated. The evaluation and change in a trust relationship, was studied in connection with reputation systems by [4, 6, 9, 11, 13]. We will integrate their work in the further practical development of this concept, for now our working assumption is that some event has caused a change in the trust into an application.

Let's assume that due to some event the Right3 of Application 8 changes to Right4.If there are no Rights explicitly mentioned for an application for a specific resource, then due to privacy reasons, security (from virus and spyware)

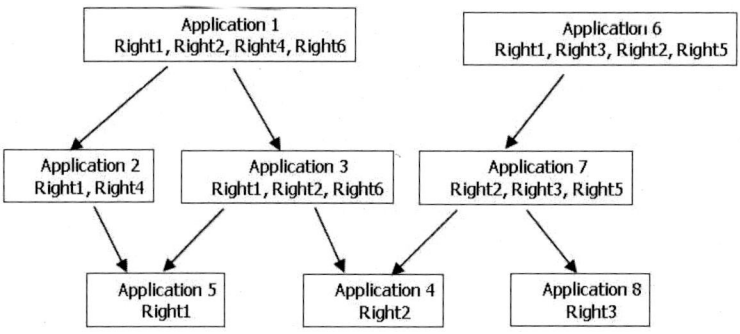

Fig. 1. Simple Example of Adaptive Trust Graph

and performance the default should be "no access". Then the position of the Application 8 in the graph changes due to the event as outlined in the example below. The trust graph can therefore reflect event orienation and change of trust over time (which is considered to be a time triggered event).

The access rights might have some dedicated sub-structure, e.g. if one application has a "write" right, then it also has a "read" right. In a more complex scenarios, the Rights might be bound to some conditions e.g. perform this transaction, if the reputation value of the transaction partner is higher than some pre-set value.

The adaptive trust graph can be grouped into context based sub-graphs based on the non-zero rights that are connected to the different resources. A group of resources build the actual user context.

For example, the user may have a banking application and a health care application running on his device. The common context elements would be e.g. name, address. Separate context elements would be for example, heart rate monitor data, account management, online username. Below we give an example, of how the rights of the different applications overlap and are linked:

Now we turn to the fact that trust is usually user context related in the sense, that applications with similar context have similar rights. The trust relationship graph outlined before, can be grouped into context based nodes, which are logically belonging to user-context groups and data sets. Below we outline, a grouping for online applications and a health application in Figure 4.

A device platform could adaptively provide a node that resides higher in the graph, in case of conflict with the "priority" rights, e.g. a health care application that is in conflict with some other application on the access to a limited resource, like network bandwidth or memory capability. Every time a resource is requested, a supporting platform could provide a check, against the rights of the applications and position in the graph with regard to the position (and connected rights) of the other applications. If some event happens, then the context based trust graph is adapted based on the nature of the event e.g. rights are changed, deleted or added. The management of the trust graph should be performed in

Table 1. Priorities for Rights

Application / Information	Banking Application	Browsing Application	Health Care Application	Health Reader	On-line Betting
Name	Access (Right3)	None	Access (Right3)	None	Access (Right3)
Address	Access (Right1)	None	Access (Right1)	None	None
Account Management	Access (Right2)	None	None	None	Access (Right2)
Online Username	None	Access (Right4)	None	None	Access (Right4)
Network Access	Access (Right5)	Access (Right5)	Access (Right5, priority)	None	Access (Right5)
Heartrate Monitor Data	None	None	Right6	Right6	None

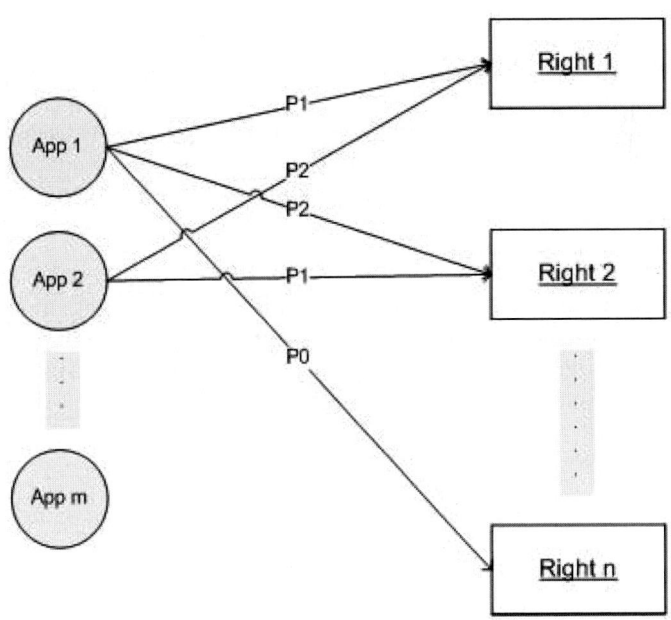

Fig. 2. Example Adaptive Trust Graph after Event

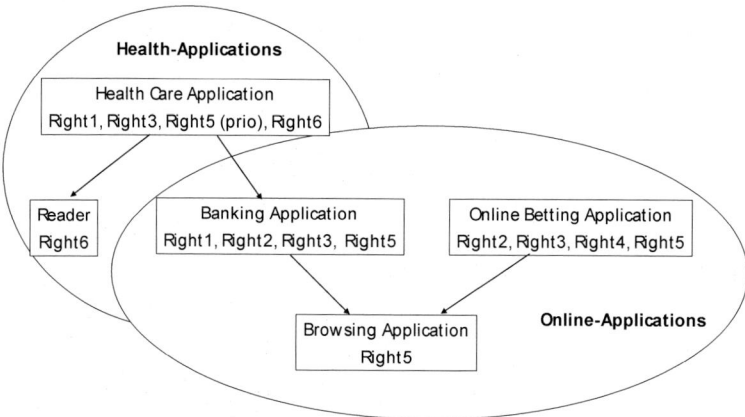

Fig. 3. : Context Aware Access Rights

a secure environment of the platform and the cause of the event should be reliable and trustworthy, but we will not elaborate on this. Our context graph has no automated means to detect non-traceable trust changing events, these are events that can not be evaluated automatically. But manual changes that are performed directly can change the trust graph. Trust can only be emulated to some degree.

5   Summary

In this article we derive from social trust scenarios a set of abstract trust properties. Based on these abstract trust properties, we derive an adaptive context-based trust graph that addresses these properties in the following manner:

– **Trust is time dynamic**

If trust is decreasing due to natural flow of time, then the rights in the nodes in the trust graph changes. These changes will result in a change of position of the node in the trust graph. This reflects the natural change of trust relationship between the different nodes.

– **Trust changes are event oriented**

An event can cause a direct change of the trust graph, in the same way as the "time-based" adaptation of the trust graph.

– **Trust can be inherited to some degree**

The structure of the trust graph reflects a certain hierarchy, in case of conflicts, the notion of "priority" is used. Recommendations can change the trust one puts into an entity in the graph. For example, the rights are connected to the condition that a reputation is over certain preset limit and this limit is reached now, then the condition is always met and the right is granted. Then the position in the trust graph is adapted accordingly.

– Trust is context based

The context-based adaptive trust graph can be grouped into context based "groups". This happens naturally through the applications and the rights / resource structure of the nodes.

– Trust can be caused / modified by non-detectable events

This is currently not reflected I the adaptive trust hierarchy, therefore we suggest that the user should have the possibility to grant explicitly access and rights e.g. on request. Not everything can be detected and solved by an automated system.

The context-aware adaptive trust concept can be applied into various areas, such as mobile applications and services, web services, ubiquitous or pervasive computing systems and resource access control . The concept reflects the social approach to trust, but it may introduce some performance bottleneck, authentication / authorization challenges and evaluation of the best rights description approach e.g. [17, 15]. These issues and the optimization and evaluation through an implementation are for further research. The actual calculation of suitable trust determining factors is also an subject for further study and will take into account work of [4, 6, 13, 11] et al.

Acknowledgement

Part of this work has been performed in the framework of the IST project System Engineering for Security and Dependability SERENITY and the ITEA Trust4All, which are partly funded by the European Union. The authors would like to acknowledge the contributions and review of their colleagues from Nokia Corporation.

References

1. Abdul-Rahman, A.,Halles S., "A Distributed Trust Model" Proc. of the 1997 New Security Paradigms Workshop, Cumbria, UK (1997), pp. 48—60.
2. Bhatti, R., Bertino, E.; Ghafoor, A., "A trust-based context-aware access control model for Web-services", Proc. of the IEEE International Conference on Web Services (2004), pp. 184 – 191.
3. Baldwin, A., Shiu, S., "Hardware Security Appliances for Trust", Proc. of the iTrust 2003.
4. Chen, M., Singh, J. P., "Computing and using reputations for internet ratings", Proc. of the Conference on Electronic Commerce EC'01, Florida, USA (2001).
5. Dey, A. K., "Understanding and Using Context", Personal and Ubiquitous Computing Journal, Volume 5 (2001), pp. 4-7.
6. Ginzboorg, P., Moloney, S., "Security for interactions in pervasive networks", Proc. Of 1st European Workshop on Security in Ad-hoc and Sensor Networks ESAS (2004).

7. Grandison, T., Sloman, M., "A Survey of Trust in Internet Applications", IEEE Communications and Survey 3 (4), (2000), pp. 2-16.
8. Hardin, R., "The street-level epistemology of trust", Politics and Society, 21 (December 1993) 4, pp. 505-529.
9. Holtmanns, S., Sarkio. K.,"Tailored Trustworthiness Estimations in Peer-to-Peer Networks", International Journal of Internet Technology and Secured Transactions (IJITST), Inderscience, to appear, (2006).
10. House, R., Rousseau, D. M., Thomas-Hunt, M., "The Meso Paradigm: A Framework for the Integration of Micro and Marco Organizational Behaviour", Research in Organizational Behaviour (1998), L. L. Cummings, B. M. Staw Eds., JAI Press, Greenwich, pp. 348 – 365.
11. Issarny, V., Liu, J., "Enhanced reputation mechanism for mobile ad-hoc networks", Proc. of iTrust Conference 2004, pp. 48 – 62.
12. Mayer, F. L., "A Brief Comparison of Two Different Environmental Guidelines for Determining 'Levels Of Trust' (Computer Security)," 6th Annual Computer Security Applications Conference (1990).
13. Moloney, M., Weber, S, "A context aware trust-based security system for ad-hoc networks", Proc. of the 1st International Conference on Security and Privacy for Emerging Areas in Communications Networks (2005).
14. Putman, R. "Bowling Alone: America's declining social capital", Journal of Democracy Vol. 6 (1995) 1, pp 64 - 78.
15. Motion Picture Expert Group (MPEG) - Rights Expression Language (REL).
16. Rousseau, D., Sitkin S., Burt R., Camerer C., "Not so Different after All: A Cross-Discipline View of Trust", Academy of Management Review 23, no. 3 (1998), pp. 393-404.
17. OASIS eXtensible Access Control Markup Language (XACML), http://www.oasis-open.org/committees/tc_home.php?wg_abbrev=xacml

Sweeper-Agent Recommendations-Tree Early Scheme

Sameh Abdel-Naby and Paolo Giorgini

Department of Information and Communication technology
University of Trento - ITALY
(sameh,paolo.giorgini)@dit.unitn.it

Abstract. This paper presents a possible roadmap for what we call a "Sweeper-Agent": an environment-friendly agents-based mobile technique, which is carried out within the activities of BlueAgents (http://dit.unitn.it/blueagents/), a newly-formed research project focusing on the integration of mobile Bluetooth communications and Agent-based applications. We foresee architecture of a service management technique that would increase the efficiency of mobile service. This paper proceeds in four sections. The first section outlines the state of the art of Agent-Oriented Architectures, and the motivation behind our research. The next section explains the Sweeper-Agent framework that uses Agent-Based Recommendations-Tree for mobile application, and how this will help mobile applications developers. Then we introduce Sweeper-Agent foreseeable integrations. And we describe the Sweeper-Agent positioning within the already implemented ToothAgent. Finally, we demonstrate the value-added service opportunity that may occur when Sweeper-Agent is implemented within mobile-agent architecture.

1 Introduction

Ambient Intelligence information systems and mobile-based applications are two promising approaches in the direction of enhancing Service-Oriented Architecture (SOA). Objects-Identification related technologies are encouraging scholars to build up Smart Ambient systems that can interact with humans and objects to improve the surrounding atmosphere. The merit goes to Sensors Technology in forming a virtual community between environmental objects. This virtual community is reasonably interactive, and it provides data that can be used forward in studying the ambient intelligence theories.

Location-based services help mobile users to achieve daily desires in a shorter and smarter way. A situation in which a mobile user in a certain area is recognized by all of the surrounding devices increases the usability of a range of resources that may have never been used before. For example, suppose a mobile user in a governmental office is asking for a driving license renewal; the recognition of the surrounding devices in the office space may help this mobile user to be informed that a new legislation is applied and could be clarified at a located office. At the same time, if coordination between agents is set up, another communication can be made to inform the mobile user that the nearby insurance company office would be interested to have a copy of the new driving license.

Our framework suggests that agents will control the process of mobile devices tracking through maintaining a history records saving method that predicts a range of random locations that a mobile user maybe moving to afterwards. For example, if an agent is able to recognize that the latest communication with a user took place within the university campus, a prediction can be formalized to assume that the user's next move will be within a specific range of locations such as the parking space or the bus stop. Accordingly, though such a prediction could make the system less reliable, by avoiding the use of the third-party technologies, such as sensors or alternative tracking devices, the framework has the advantage of being technically simpler and cost-effective.

This paper is structured as follows; Section.2 explains the Sweeper-Agent framework that uses Agent-Based Recommendations-Tree for mobile application. Section.3 introduces Sweeper-Agent foreseeable integrations. Section.4 describes the Sweeper-Agent positioning within the already implemented ToothAgent. Section.5 demonstrates the newly found opportunities after Sweeper-Agent.

2   Sweeper-Agent

To explain how Sweeper-Agent technique would work, we imagine the situation of a student mobile-user who is moving within the university campus, from entering to the university, reading in the library to attending a lecture in a classroom. At the same time, we assume that the university has got distributed servers able to recognize the student's moves and make a certain communication with that user. We also assume a that Sweeper-Agent works within a Used-Books offering system, ToothAgent [3], that is able to communicate with mobile users through a Bluetooth connection and exchange useful information corresponding to a student's interests. (Figure 1)

As long as the student is moving and recognized by these distributed servers, a connection record is always updated and referring to the user's new location. Also, a little but feasible time-to-live (TTL) is added to each updated request, which makes the system obliged to search automatically for the student's new location and update with the new status. Whenever the user is not found within the area that servers cover, a request is passed to the prediction server carrying the Master Sweeper-Agent, in this case - univ-sweeper-agent, and therefore a range of predictions is realized and, consequently, the request is forwarded to the nearby connected agents. (Figure 2)

Notably, Sweeper-Agent is to have a hierarchy of agents, as in each area there is a master Sweeper-Agent and a sub-Sweeper-Agent. For example, univ-sweeper-agent, that controls the routing of the requests between the university community and the predicting servers; if a student is not located in any of the university areas, this master agent will forward the service request to the predicting servers clarifying the new situation, and the prediction servers decide

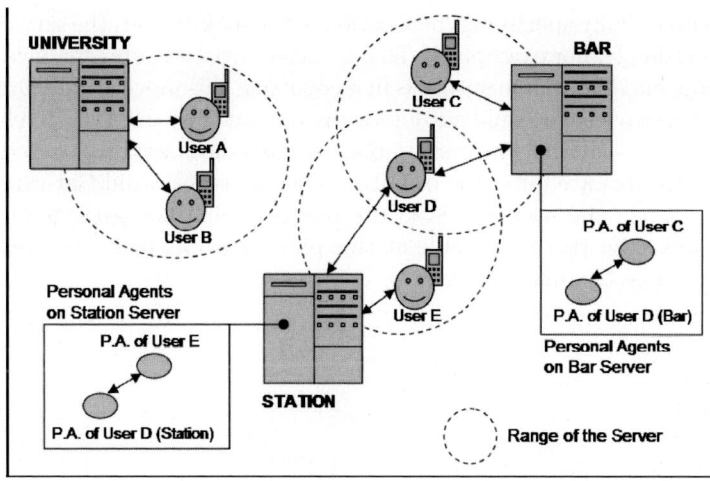

Fig. 1. Users, servers, and virtual communities of personal agents.[3]

the step ahead or the "where to go" for a service request, defining its path (Figure 3).

A worthwhile risk is taken, as the mobile user may decide to go to a point out of the coverage area, and this will lead the system to a user status recognition failure. Then the mobile-based side of the system will inform the user that a connection can not be established with any of the surrounding servers and, consequently, the service is not available at this point. But this defect could be avoided by identifying a quite wide variety of points that a user would move to after doing a certain action within the coverage areas.

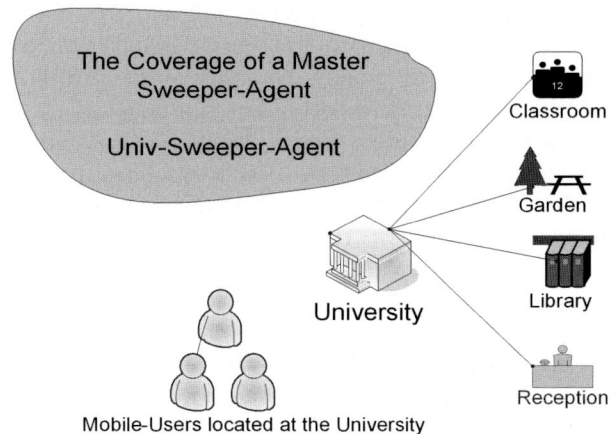

Fig. 2. Sweeper-Agent Classification.

After successfully specifying the location of the mobile user, the service can be offered accordingly. For example, if the user moves from the university campus to the bus stop, and the system succeeds in recognizing this move, a categorized pre-defined services package would automatically be routed to the user. To elaborate, when the user is in the university area, the assigned services offered by the system to this area are both, the used-books selling service and Car-ride sharing possibility. When the user moves to the bus stop, another package of services would be linked to the user profile at this point, such as bus-pass subscription renewal and new bus line schedule.

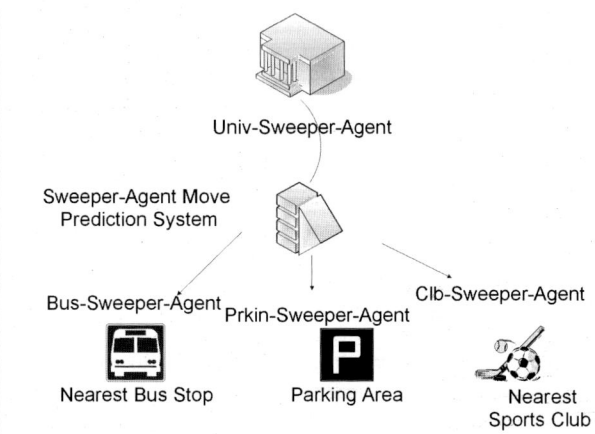

Fig. 3. Sweeper-Agent Hierarchy.

Categorizing services that could be offered in a certain location is an enhancement that will facilitate the work of mobile-based applications developers. That is because service realization perspective will be taken into account in offering the requested services packages of a specific mobile user without adding any extra developing tools that usually increase the size of the Agent and are time-consuming.

Sweeper-Agents will constitute a tree of pre-defined recommendation paths that a services request (SR) within a network will be following in order to achieve the delegated task. Each of these tree branches will, first, test itself for fulfilling this SR and in case of a negative result; this branch will pass the same SR to the approaching one, and so on until a positive feedback is given by one branch/Agent.

For a branch to achieve a service request, there are a number of steps that should be taken before the real execution of the SR. For example, once the SR reaches an achieving point, the responsible branch would broadcast its capability to implement this SR, and this broadcasting process would be a bottom-up approach using the same path that the incoming request used. This will help the dedication of the network capacity at the branch level to one request; therefore the result can be carried back faster to the mobile user. Yet, in case the mobile user is out of the coverage area, then the SR will be touring within network nodes endlessly. To solve this problem, we recommend adding a second layer "customized" TTL for each SR to reduce the inappropriate utilization of the traffic, and ensure that the SR result - indicating that the mobile user is out of the coverage area - will be returned to the system.

3   Foreseeable Integration

The ToothAgent [3] architecture is a multi-agent platform that can be installed on a server where Multi-agent techniques are enabled; each server handles a specific data service area, and system users can contact their personal agents using their Bluetooth integrated devices. Notably, ToothAgent is domain and technology-independent, so specific services provided by a server do not affect the system, and different technologies can be used in different environments.

When a mobile device user gets closer to one of the servers (Figure 1), the pre-installed software on the mobile device sets up a connection with these servers and broadcasts requests related to the accessible services. These requests depend on the previously communicated file between mobile device user and PC. Then agents try to broadcast their requests in the network in search for other agents that carry similar interests or matching criteria requests, and once a fulfilling agent was found, the results are stored locally in the ToothAgent database server. Notably, each of the allocated servers is operating throughout a Multi-agent platform. Consequently, communication among agents and mobile devices is based on one-to-one communication protocol, in a way that allows receiving and processing requests obtained by users. Distinction between agents is realized through the unique Bluetooth address of the corresponding address [3]. Finally, results are sent back to the user and a list of all visited servers that cooperated with this service is saved to be reviewed by user later on.

Figure 4 shows ToothAgent service accessing architecture. In steps 1-3 the user outline servers and services registered to the ToothAgent Database. In step 4, the user selects the more desirable services and provides the system with relevant information. In step 5, using a Bluetooth, previous data and configurations saved in the configuration file are retrieved by the mobile device. In steps 6-7, the user approaches an architecture-related server, so device software connect to it and start sending service requests upon the available ones. In steps 8-12, a pre-qualification process is initiated to confirm that the user's interests match the server services and then results are sent back to user. Finally, the mobile device is storing server addresses to record previously interacted servers.

4   Sweeper-Agent Positioning

We imagine a scenario where the mobile user X approaches a university campus that is covered by ToothAgent service servers. In the way in, X passes by the university reception, his mobile device will communicate with the location-server

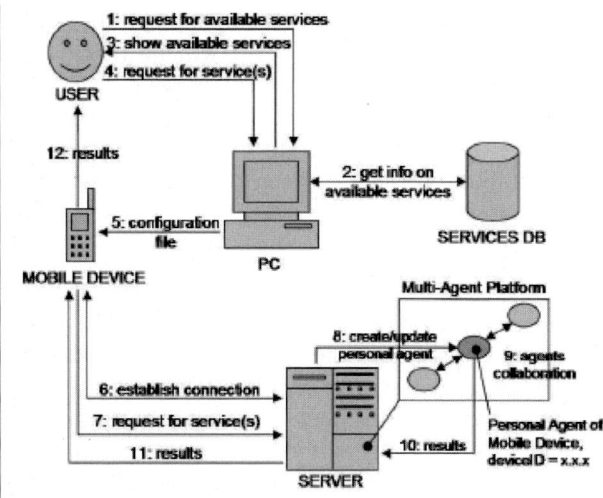

Fig. 4. ToothAgent Technique in getting access to service [3].

and uploading the pre-saved service queries or receiving previously requested data. Afterwards, X moves to the library or the classroom, and yet the location-based different servers still communicating with X's "mobile device" and refresh his/her position within the network. Notably, X's moves are restricted within the Bluetooth coverage range and whenever X leaves the Bluetooth-covered area, the connection with the offered services will be broken

Nonetheless, one of the previously proposed ways toward the extension of the coverage in such systems is to embed a network of sensors [1] that is able to identify the user's location and report it to a data-gathering server. These proposed architectures are quiet effective in mapping the user's moves - using RFID-Tags and Readers (Figure 5), for example - and, accordingly, provide a service related to his location. At the same time, and apart from the existing sensors-power-consumption problem, the disadvantage of using a network of sensors is the high cost of its embedding and maintenance. Moreover, determining the user's location does not necessarily mean that the system is able to offer him a certain service unless another layer of location-based servers are there to communicate with the user's mobile device and exchange service queries.

Therefore, Sweeper-Agent, in a scenario similar to the one of ToothAgent and taking into consideration the need of to have the above-noted extra layer of servers, will be executed/created whenever the user is not located within a network. In a hierarchal design, the master agent, "Top Agent", will be informed that a user is out of the coverage area whenever a refreshment process (pinging) happens and there is no response from the user's mobile device. The ToothAgent service server will invoke a Sweeper-Agent and send it to the prediction server; the prediction server will first review its issuer name, the Top-Agent responsible for the issuance, and accordingly forward the Sweeper-Agent to the pre-defined prediction path.

Once the user is found at any of the predicted path sites, the sweeper-agent will be back again to the ToothAgent service server and a new-place notification process will be launched. Then an old service update will be communicated with the user or a new service can be offered according to the new location. Accordingly, we will avoid the use of new hardware layer, i.e., network of sensors, while achieving the optimum utilization of the network bandwidth. That is because a service package will not be transferred within a single network unless a sweeper-agent reports the successful positioning of a mobile user; otherwise, the sweeper-agent TTL will be invoked and the request will be ignored until further communication with the user.

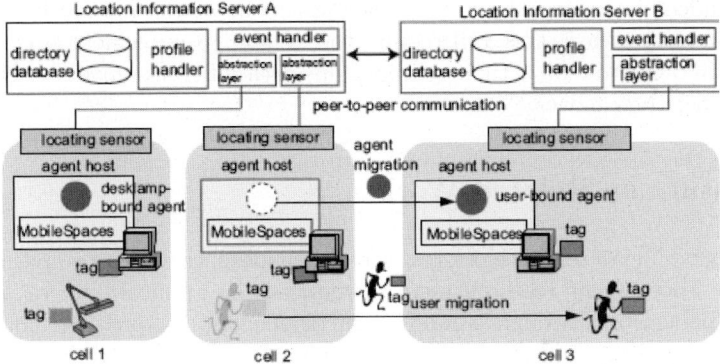

Fig. 5. Architecture of the SpatialAgent framework [1].

5   New Opportunities

Applying Sweeper-Agent in a network of mobile-users, this will allow the central system to provide users with services that are not useful, unless a user is located at a specific spot and time. For example, a user that is moving from the university and going to the bus stop, and the system has succeeded to identify the user location at the time that another user is moving to the parking area and the system, now, is able to identify both users location perfectly and report their exiting status to the central system, university-sweeper-agent, a possible implementation here is; the link between the two users and matching their destination for Car-ride sharing service.

Car sharing is a method to reduce the usage of cars in a specific town or territory, reducing car usage helps in turn to decrease pollution and prevent some other related problems. This usually takes place by having 1) a car owner who uses his/her car to move from a place to another, and 2) another person who is interested to go somewhere along the car owner's path to destination, and at the same time the ride seeker is willing to share the ride cost with the car owner.

That will be achieved easily using a Sweeper-Agent based architecture, as the car owner location will be immediately recognized as a PARKING AREA and the ride seeker location will be immediately recognized as Bus-Stop, therefore, a possible suggestions by the predictions server can be previously stored, which may lead both system users to finally share the trip to a specific destination.

Other similar services can be seen as a new opportunity for providing more feasible benefits for mobile users. For example, a university student that is located by the system at the central university library, down town, and another student that is located in a remote library and looking for book that can be hardly found. A smart matching between the two students can lead the downtown student to deliver the book to the other one at the remote library. Definitely, in such a case, this will require the system to implement user/students profiles in order to realize their relationships with different university campuses, and predict their moves.

6   Future an Related Work

ToothAgent [3] is a related work to our research ideas, as we see a convention with the way ToothAgent research team introduced the applicability for a mobile-based application, through a multi-agent framework, to provide mobile users with used-books selling service. Another related work was introduced in March '05, MoPiDig [4], this technique was applied the best within organizations that users-grouping and service-categorization is needed (e.g., museums).

A previously proposed framework, SpatialAgent [1], aiming at providing services for mobile users based on their locations, utilized a RFID-based location model, Radio Frequency Identifications, to identify objects and users locations, and a location-information-servers (LISs) to manage location sensing systems and agent devices. In this system, agents have a graphical interface that allows their interaction with users who can freely customize them. A related research, "follow-me" [2], conducted by Cambridge University's Sentient Computing Project, assumed that a space is equipped with tracking systems that help the location identification process of users and objects

Some of the topics we are planning to focus on in our future research are: (1) Implementing a Sweeper-Agent-enabled version of the ToothAgent, and test it in different situations providing different kinds of services, e.g., car-ride sharing in case the user is by the bus stop; (2) Learning Agents, as the research area that is going to increase the smartness level of agents to understand the mobile users common visiting zones and timings, and accordingly, leading the system to faster predictions; (3) Integrating a smart approach for users to search services in a menu-based style, in which we see a significant potential, as it will give users the possibility to search services linked to other locations for planning or knowledge reasons and finally (4), Agents-Customization technique, introducing the ability for a user to customize the services categories and select only the ones he is interested in.

7   Conclusions

This paper introduced the early scheme of Sweeper-Agent, a new technique used for providing a location-based services, this arise when a pre-defined list of locations installed on a prediction server is considered, this list assumes the availability of a mobile-user at specific location after being in another one. We showed that this technique can be implemented within a Multi-agent based architectures in order to facilitate the mission of service packages transfer within a network and ensure a good utilization of the bandwidth. Then we demonstrated the possibility or Sweeper-Agent to integrate with ToothAgent, an already implemented and tested architecture for selling and offering used books among students at university of Trento, Italy. Finally, we illustrated a scenario where RFID technology is used to determine user locations, and then we positioned Sweeper-Agent in the same architecture so we avoid the use of any sensors framework.

Acknowledgments

We first thank the University of Trento - BlueAgents Research Group for the efforts made to carry out a different promising research activities. In particular, we thank ToothAgent research team and ArsLogica s.r.l. for the unabated cooperation and support given to innovative and creative ideas

References

1. Ichiro Satoh: Mobile Agents for Ambient Intelligence, Proceedings of MMAS 2004: Kyoto, Japan, pp. 187-201..
2. A. Harter, A. Hopper, P. Steggeles, A. Ward, and P. Webster: The Anatomy of a Context-Aware Application, Proceedings of Conference on Mobile Computing and Networking (MOBICOM'99), pp. 59-68, ACM Press, 1999.
3. Bryl, Volha and Giorgini, Paolo and Fante, Stefano (2005) Toothagent: a Multi-Agent System for Virtual Communities Support. Technical Report DIT-05-064, Informatica e Telecomunicazioni, University of Trento.
4. Seitz, C., Berger, M., Bauer B. "MoPiDiG" , Proceedings of the First International Workshop on Mobile Peer-to-Peer Computing, Orlando, Florida, USA, Mrz 2004.

Which cooperation / competition issues for AmI stakeholders

Jacques Bus

Head of Unit, D4 - ICT for Trust and Security DG Information Society, European Commission

Extended Abstract

In the coming years, and this AmI.d conference will be proof of it, we may witness technology breakthroughs towards the provision of Ambient Intelligence (AmI) in our daily lives. The increasing convergence between computing, communications and broadcasting with the emergence of RFID, geospatial and location-based technologies, sensor networking and further miniaturisation, leads to what many call AmI.

From a networking perspective one sees concepts like the "Internet of things", "Ubiquitous sensor networks" or simply of the "Future Internet". From the service and software perspective the focus is on a "Service-centric Information Society". For researchers in micro and nano electronics and computing the view is on quasi-infinite storage and computing power made available through pervasive computing and storage grids.

From the perspective of the users however, security, privacy, interoperability and ease of use will be highest on the agenda. Dependability and security of the devices, networks and systems, and trustworthiness of easy-to-use services delivered by these will ultimately determine the acceptance of AmI by the citizens.

The convergence and integration aspects of AmI demonstrate the need for cooperation at many levels. Researchers from many different disciplines will have to work together to reach the needed breakthroughs at the technology level, as well as to ensure acceptance by society of the products and processes made available by the technology. Industries have to cooperate to agree on the much needed standardisation and interoperability, which up till now have appeared to be essential stumble blocks for broad acceptance of high technology devices by consumers. Governments must talk together to restore stability in the international legal environment for businesses, consumers and to ensure national security in a world run by AmI.

For example, the security risks of the current Internet for the proper functioning of the public critical infrastructures require intensive cooperation between networking (wired and wireless) and security experts to develop resilient (dependable, self-recovering and -healing, "intelligent") networks and systems, which can make our future AmI world sustainable.

Another example of much required cooperation of many stakeholders that can be given is Identity and Privacy management. Here we see a plethora of developments: processors (RFID, TPM), biometrics, contact-less smart cards, data protection and security, privacy enhancing technologies and services, legal and regulatory problems (also in the international context) and social problems (protection against crime and privacy abuse), which all need our attention in a coordinated fashion to ensure an AmI world that supports our societal values.

But many other examples can and will be discussed in the conference.

AmI has great potential for European industry and research to take a lead in many promising new entrepreneurial activities with innovative products and processes. Europe has a strong position in systems and complexity research, software engineering, mobile networking, consumer electronics, biometrics, smart cards and TPMs. Europe has also strong expertise in (multi-cultural) services, privacy matters, data protection regulation and building a society based on liberty and societal values. Finally, Europe has strong strategic interests to protect and extend its societal values by developing technologies for security, trust and privacy in a future AmI world.

To build a Service-oriented Information Society that will deliver growth and prosperity, we need to tailor information and communication technologies to business and social needs, and ensure that they become useful tools for economic and social innovation. Using its research and industrial capabilities and developing its strategic interests, Europe may bring the prosperity expected to come with AmI through healthy competition and intelligent cooperation

The seventh Framework Programme for Community Research, in particular the theme on Information and Communication Technologies will focus on stimulating the process of integration and inter-disciplinary research, with the aim to improve European competitiveness world-wide and build a sustainable Information Society in Europe.

Ambient Intelligence and Open Innovation

Emile Aarts

Philips Research

Extended Abstract

Although originally developed by Philips as a novel paradigm for consumer electronics, the vision of ambient intelligence should not be regarded as a Philips controlled concept. Major efforts enrolled by the European Commission have led to the support of the vision by many industrial and academic partners in an open context, thus allowing Europe to regain a major competitive position in the world.

The vision and its origin. Ambient Intelligence articulates a novel paradigm for consumer electronics for the years beyond 2010. It was developed in the late nineties of the past century in a series of internal workshops, which were commissioned by the Philips board of management Philips, and that led to a vision of a world of fully integrated, user-friendly smart surroundings supporting well-being, self-expression, and productivity. This vision has developed over the past years into a solid basis for the company's Lifestyle strategy, and to the brand campaign Sense and Simplicity that builds on the three-way customer promise called designed around you, easy to experience, and advanced, which is an excellent way of explaining ambient intelligence to people in the streets. It has contributed substantially to the new product creation process inside Philips; groundbreaking examples are the Active AmBi Light TV and The Ambient Experience.

Opening up the vision. Following the advise of the Information Society and Technology Advisory Group (ISTAG) issued in 2001, The European Commission used the vision for the launch of their 6th framework program (FP6) in Information, Society, and Technology (IST), with a subsidiary budget of 3.7 billion Euro. As a consequence many new initiatives were launched throughout Europe. Fraunhofer Gesellschaft embraced the concept and originated activities in a variety of domains including multimedia, micro-systems design and augmented spaces. Their InHaus project is similar to Philips' HomeLab and can be viewed as the Fraunhofer Gesellschafts approach to user centered design. Several over five million Euro research programs on ambient intelligence were started at national levels in a large variety of countries including, Germany, Italy, Spain, France, and The Netherlands. Very promising in this respect are the ideas centered around the concepts of Experience and Application Research which is aimed at the development of facilities that conduct research into user behavior and end-user design. Finally, we mention that over the years the Philips originated European Symposium on Ambient Intelligence (EUSAI), has grown into a major event for the exchange of novel ideas in Ambient Intelligence.

Open innovation. Awareness has grown over the years that the classical approach to industrial research can no longer provide the technological innovation required to drive the world's economical development. New models for industrial research have been proposed that build on the ideas of the networked knowledge economy using the concept of Open Innovation. This concept is based on the belief that tapping into as many as possible bright people can develop more innovative ideas, and in doing so, industrial research needs to widen its scope to become more collaborative and open-minded. Ambient Intelligence has been quite instrumental in the realization of open innovation. We mention three major initiatives. The AMI@Work group combines parties from both the public and the private domains to provide a forum for the discussion of the use of Ambient Intelligence in daily life. This has led to a major research program in the domain of Future and Emerging Technologies called Ambient Assisted Living, which has been proposed for FP7. The European Technology Platform Artemis for the development of embedded systems builds on the Ambient Intelligence visions to define and deploy their strategic research agenda. In addition to these public-private initiatives there are also exclusively private initiatives that are aimed at international collaboration. The Ambient Intelligence Research and Development (AIR&D) consortium in which INRIA, Fraunhofer Gesellschaft, Philips, and Thompson jointly develop middleware for Ambient Intelligence is a very productive example.

For Philips Research many of the initiatives mentioned above have played a major role in the development and implementation of their vision of Ambient Intelligence, and first business successes have been reported. Nevertheless, we also feel that the vision has to enter a next stage in its development as our insights in Lifestyle are deepening and the request is becoming louder to come up with solutions that can live up to the Ambient Intelligence promise of making life more easy. These can indeed be realized in a number of new areas such as learning and education, ambient assisted living, and hospitality. To provide Europe with a competitive edge in these domains it is imperative that the best in class partner to drive business innovation in a truly open manner.

Author Index

Achevé d'imprimer sur les presses de l'Imprimerie BARNÉOUD
B.P. 44 - 53960 BONCHAMP-LÈS-LAVAL
Dépôt légal : septembre 2006 - N° d'imprimeur : 609020
Imprimé en France